The Abandoned Empress

3

INA

Original Story by
Yuna

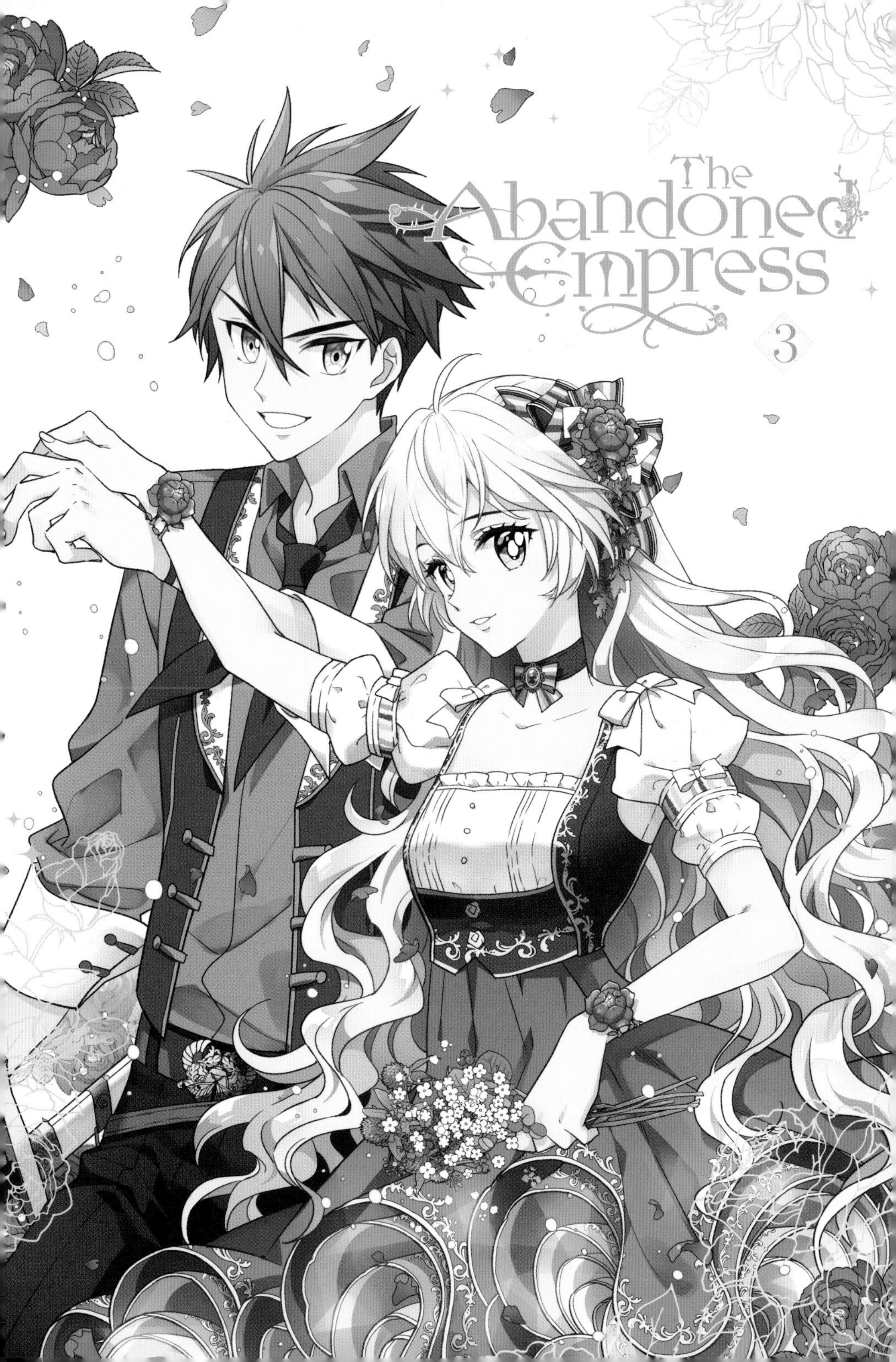
The Abandoned Empress
3

The Abandoned Empress

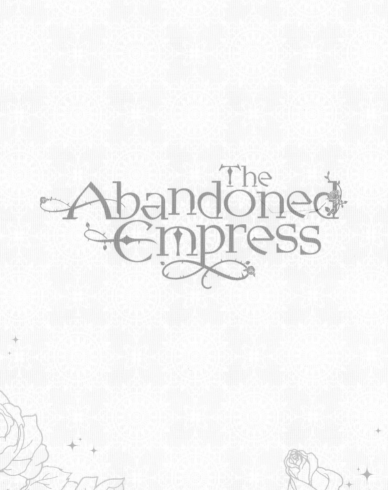

YOUR HIGHNESS, WON'T YOU CONSIDER RESTING YOUR EYES A LITTLE WHILE?

UGH...

EVERY INCH OF MY DESK IS COVERED WITH MATTERS THAT REQUIRE MY ATTENTION—HOW AM I TO REST?

BUT SIRE, YOU'VE BEEN WORKING NONSTOP THESE DAYS.

...THE WHOLE CONTINENT IS IN TUMULT THIS YEAR.

THE CHANCELLOR IS AWAY ON THE RELIEF MISSION, THE BORDER REGIONS ARE RATHER UNSTABLE, AND THE CITIZENS ARE ANXIOUS.

I FEAR IT MAY IMPACT YOUR HEALTH AT THIS RATE.

AT SUCH A TIME, LEAVING MATTERS TO OTHERS IS OUT OF THE QUESTION.

ABOVE ALL, THIS IS A TASK HIS MAJESTY SAW FIT TO ENTRUST TO ME. IT'S NOT SOMETHING I CAN NEGLECT.

... UNDERSTOOD. WELL SAID, SIRE.

ANNOUN—

SHWIP

PAT

PAT

HO-HO!

IS SOMEONE ELSE 'IN THERE...?

BUT THEN, YOUNG LADY, YOU SEEM QUITE PALE. ARE YOU PERHAPS UNWELL?

I'VE BEEN SOMEWHAT OUT OF SORTS, YOUR MAJESTY. MY APOLOGIES FOR APPEARING BEFORE YOU IN SUCH A STATE.

SO SHE'S HERE?

HAD WE BUT KNOWN YOU WERE UNWELL, WE'D HAVE SUGGESTED A LATER DATE. THIS IS MOST REGRETTABLE ON OUR PART.

WE SHALL DISPATCH THE COURT PHYSICIAN FOR YOU.

AND DO REGARD IT AS AN IMPERIAL ORDER, NOT TO BE REJECTED.

...I THANK YOU FOR YOUR GENEROSITY, YOUR MAJESTY.

WE HOPE TO SOON SEE OUR ESTEEMED YOUNG LADY WELL RECOVERED!

HO·HO!

......

...ANNOUNCE ME.

YES, YOUR HIGH-NESS.

ANNOUNCING THE CROWN PRINCE!!

HAVE YOU CALLED FOR ME, YOUR MAJESTY?

YES, GREETINGS, YOUNG PRINCE.

MM...WE WERE HOPING TO HAVE TEA TOGETHER, BUT IT SEEMS SHE IS UNWELL.

OH... YOUR MAJESTY, PLEASE DON'T MIND ME...

NO, NO. WE CANNOT TROUBLE ONE WHO IS ILL.

HMM... AH, YES!

YOUNG PRINCE, YOU WOULDN'T MIND ESCORTING THE YOUNG LADY, YES?

WE SHALL HAVE THE TEA PREPARED FOR YOUR RETURN.

UNDERSTOOD, YOUR MAJESTY.

TH-THAT'S NOT NECESSARY, YOUR MAJESTY!

THERE'S NO NEED TO GO TO SUCH LENGTHS...!

...THEN I SHALL TAKE MY LEAVE, YOUR MAJESTY.

WE WISH YOU A SWIFT RECOVERY, MOST ESTEEMED YOUNG LADY.

I'M HAVING TROUBLE BREATHING...

MY CONDITION'S GOTTEN WORSE.

JUST ENDURE A BIT MORE.

IT'LL BE FINE ONCE I'M OUT OF HERE.

AND DON'T LET HIM SEE YOU STRUGGLE.

THANK YOU FOR SEEING ME OFF, YOUR HIGHNESS. I'LL TAKE MY LEAVE—

SIR LANKH!

......

YES, YOUR HIGHNESS!

HAVE A CARRIAGE BROUGHT AROUND.

WE'RE GOING TO THE MONIQUE ESTATE.

?!

RATTLE
RATTLE

HUH?! BUT I THOUGHT HE HATED EVEN THE SIGHT OF ME...!

AH...MAYBE THAT'S IT. THE EMPEROR DIDN'T SPECIFY JUST HOW FAR HE SHOULD ESCORT ME.

HE'S TAKING ME ALL THE WAY HOME IN ORDER TO MAKE SURE NOBODY CAN FIND FAULT WITH HIM.

......

BY THE LOOK ON HER FACE, SHE COULD COLLAPSE AT ANY MOMENT.

YET SHE MANAGED TO ARRIVE FOR HER AUDIENCE.

ON TOP OF THAT, SHE COMPOSED HERSELF PERFECTLY.

IF SHE'S FIVE YEARS YOUNGER THAN ME, SHE'LL HAVE TURNED TWELVE THIS YEAR.

SHE'S EXTREMELY RESOLUTE DESPITE HER AGE.

AS BELOVED BY THE EMPEROR AS YOU ARE...

...EVEN IF YOU CHOSE TO REST, YOUR ACTIONS WOULD HAVE BEEN EXCUSED.

...WHAT FOOLS WE ARE...

...BOTH YOU... AND I.

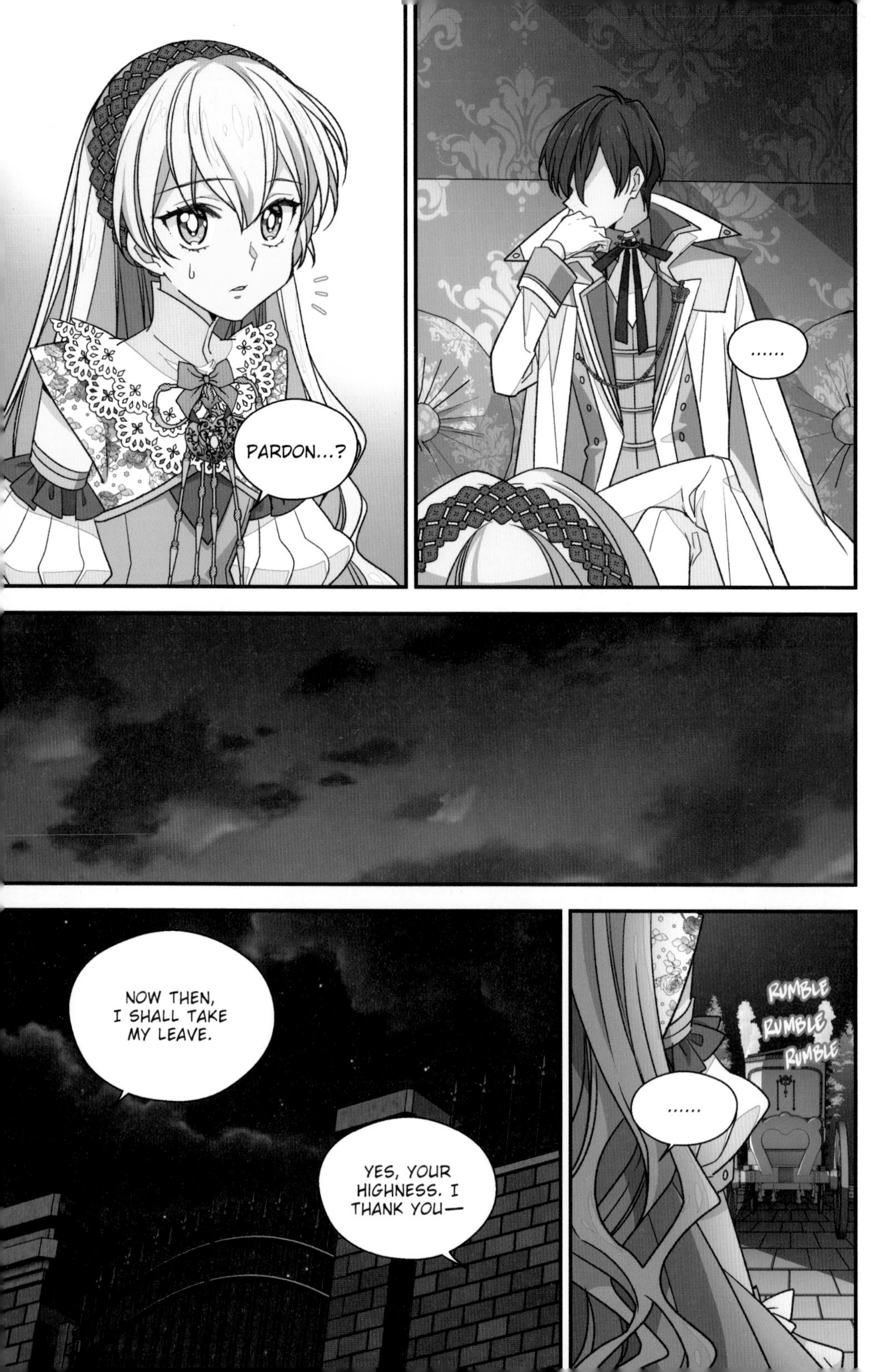
PARDON...?
......
NOW THEN, I SHALL TAKE MY LEAVE.
YES, YOUR HIGHNESS. I THANK YOU—
RUMBLE
RUMBLE
RUMBLE
......

...WHAT IS THIS? THAT WASN'T HOW I EXPECTED IT TO GO.

I'D WANTED TO FLEE FROM HIM ONLY A SHORT WHILE AGO.

...WHAT FOOLS WE ARE...

COULD IT BE...

...THAT HE BROUGHT ME HOME OUT OF CONCERN...?

......

WHAT AM I THINKING?!

IT COULD NEVER BE THAT! NOT WHEN HE HATES ME AS MUCH AS HE DOES!

HONESTLY... WHAT A NONSENSICAL THING TO IMAGINE.

THE REASON...

...THAT I DIDN'T FEEL SO AFRAID OF HIM TODAY...

...IS BECAUSE I WAS PREOCCUPIED WITH NOT COLLAPSING, SO I COULDN'T TAKE ENOUGH NOTICE OF HIS MOOD.

THAT MUST BE IT...

WE HOPE TO
SOON SEE...

...OUR ESTEEMED
YOUNG LADY WELL
RECOVERED!

TMP...

FROM THIS MOMENT, WE SHALL WATCH OVER YOU AROUND THE CLOCK, MY LADY.

AROUND THE CLOCK?

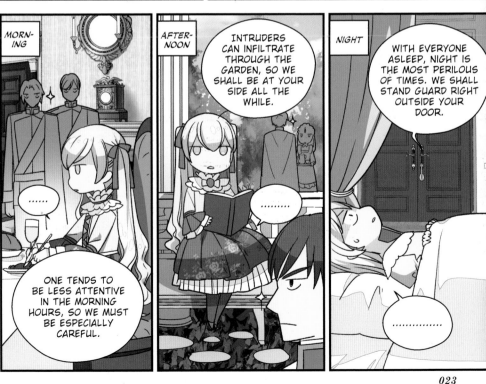

MORN-ING

ONE TENDS TO BE LESS ATTENTIVE IN THE MORNING HOURS, SO WE MUST BE ESPECIALLY CAREFUL.

......

AFTER-NOON

INTRUDERS CAN INFILTRATE THROUGH THE GARDEN, SO WE SHALL BE AT YOUR SIDE ALL THE WHILE.

....

NIGHT

WITH EVERYONE ASLEEP, NIGHT IS THE MOST PERILOUS OF TIMES. WE SHALL STAND GUARD RIGHT OUTSIDE YOUR DOOR.

....

THIS IS RATHER SUFFOCATING.

I COULDN'T GET THIS KIND OF PROTECTION... EVEN AS AN IMPERIAL CONSORT...

I'VE NEVER BEEN SO CLOSELY GUARDED BEFORE...

...AND YET I'M RECEIVING THIS TREATMENT DESPITE NOT BEING A MEMBER OF THE IMPERIAL FAMILY JUST YET.

WHAT IRONY.

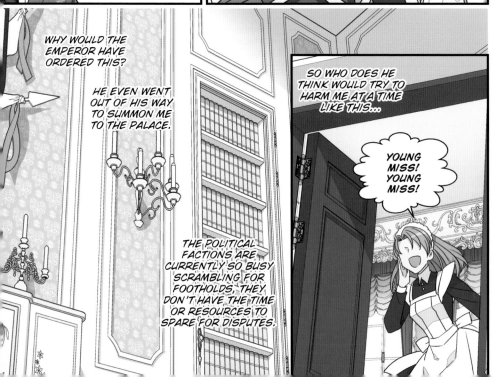

WHY WOULD THE EMPEROR HAVE ORDERED THIS?

HE EVEN WENT OUT OF HIS WAY TO SUMMON ME TO THE PALACE.

THE POLITICAL FACTIONS ARE CURRENTLY SO BUSY SCRAMBLING FOR FOOTHOLDS, THEY DON'T HAVE THE TIME OR RESOURCES TO SPARE FOR DISPUTES.

SO WHO DOES HE THINK WOULD TRY TO HARM ME AT A TIME LIKE THIS...

YOUNG MISS! YOUNG MISS!

YOU'VE GOT MAIL!

THERE'S SOMETHING FROM THE YOUNG LORD VERITA!

JUST WHAT THE YOUNG MISS WAS WAITING FOR!

!!

THERE ARE TWO.

SCURRY SCURRY

THIS PALE-GREEN STATIONERY... ALLENDIS...!

To My
Dearly Missed
Young Lady...

It's been so long.
I'm sorry for not being
in touch. We've been
continuously on the
move, and we just arrived
at a larger territory.

We're now
dispatching
soldiers to the
surrounding villages
to inform people
we're distributing
provisions.

We had been
expecting the worst,
but thankfully, it's
not as severe as we
had imagined.

We thoroughly
prepared for this,
so if the nation can
make it through this
winter, the situation
should see some
improvement.

Though, the relief
efforts will need
to be kept up for
several years going
forward.

Have you been well?

As you've been left alone there, I'm most regretful I cannot be by your side.

You always exude strength, but I know that you're a delicate soul and quite prone to loneliness.

Even if you'd never admit it.

Don't go overboard in your efforts and mind your health well.

I'll write to you again.

From your knight in shining armor, Allendis.

OH, ALLENDIS... YOU'RE ALWAYS SO SWEET.

I CAN FEEL YOUR WARMTH THROUGH THE PAPER.

LET'S SEE WHO SENT ME THE OTHER LETTER......HM?

To my daughter, Tia. Greetings from the South, from your father.

PAPA...!!

IT'S A LETTER FROM PAPA!!

IS HE WELL?! I DIDN'T THINK HE'D WRITE TO ME...!

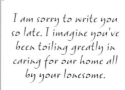

I am sorry to write you so late. I imagine you've been toiling greatly in caring for our home all by your lonesome.

Is your training going well? I've been worried, thinking back on how impatient you seemed to be.

SO PAPA WAS AWARE...

Just in case my worries are warranted, I shall say this—

There is no need for such urgency, my dear Tia.

Your father is ready to give you help at any time.

If you so desire, we shall spare no means nor method...

...in granting whatever it is you wish.

You're doing well enough, so believe in yourself and let your mind be more at ease.

PAPA...!!!

I TRULY AM A FOOL! PAPA HAS BEEN WORRIED FOR ME AND BEEN SUPPORTING ME AT EVERY STEP ALL ALONG...!

AND INSTEAD OF BELIEVING HE WAS, I JUST TRIED TO DO IT ALL ON MY OWN...

PAPA... ALLENDIS...

I MISS YOU...

SIR SEYMORE— A MOMENT OF YOUR TIME, IF YOU PLEASE.

YES?

...?!

MY LADY, THOSE CLOTHES ARE...?

COULD YOU HELP ME WITH SOMETHING?

INSTEAD OF YOU JUST STANDING GUARD ALL DAY LONG...

I'D LIKE YOU TO TEACH ME THE WAYS OF THE SWORD.

...I PROPOSE WE MAKE BETTER USE OF OUR TIME TOGETHER.

YES, LET'S CURB MY IMPATIENCE.

I'LL START OVER WITH A NEW MINDSET.

I'LL TAKE EACH STEP SLOWLY AND GIVE IT MY ALL.

THAT IS HOW...

...I SHALL RETURN THE FAVOR TO MYSELF AND THOSE I TREASURE WHO'VE BELIEVED IN ME ALWAYS.

YOU'RE STILL UP? WE'RE DOING MORE INSPECTIONS TOMORROW, FIRST THING IN THE MORNING...

I SHALL NOT BE A HINDRANCE TO OUR WORK, SO YOU DO NOT NEED TO GO OUT OF YOUR WAY TO CHECK UP ON ME, SIR.

......

IT SEEMS YOU STILL HAVE COMPLAINTS AFTER COMING ALL THIS WAY, THEN.

ALEXIS IS UNWELL, SO SHOULD IT NOT FALL TO YOU, HIS YOUNGER BROTHER, TO COMPLETE THIS TASK?

YOUR COMING WAS ORDERED BY THE EMPEROR HIMSELF, SO EXERCISE SOME OBEDIENCE.

......

THIS IS ALL A RESULT OF YOUR OWN MAKING.

YOUR LINGERING ABOUT THE GIRL WHO IS CURRENTLY THE ONE CROWN-PRINCESS-TO-BE...

...REACHED HIS MAJESTY'S EARS, AND SO YOU'VE BEEN OUSTED HERE.

...I DO ACKNOWLEDGE THAT I MIGHT HAVE OVERSTEPPED.

BUT WHILE YOU MIGHT SAY THAT, FATHER...

...AM I MISTAKEN IN THINKING YOU'RE OF THE SAME THOUGHT AS ME?

WELL— I SUPPOSE YOU'D RATHER IT WERE SOMEONE OTHER THAN ME.

...DO NOT SPEAK SO CARELESSLY, ALLENDIS.

ONE WRONG WORD FROM YOU COULD BRAND THE ENTIRETY OF OUR HOUSE AS TRAITORS.

SET ASIDE YOUR USELESS NOTIONS AND GO TO SLEEP.

...I'M THE ONE WHO PUT IN ALL THE HARD WORK—

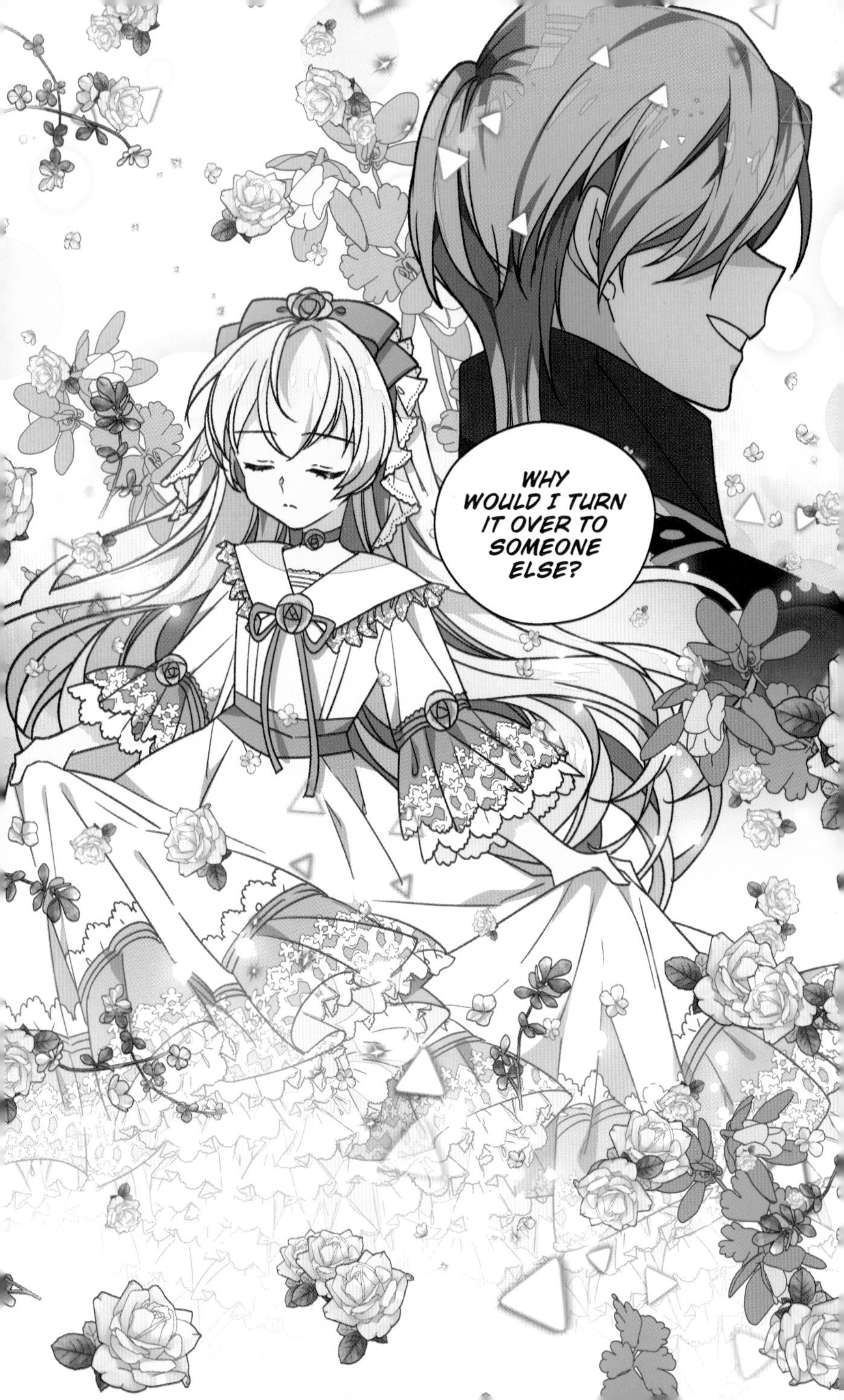
WHY WOULD I TURN IT OVER TO SOMEONE ELSE?

The Abandoned Empress

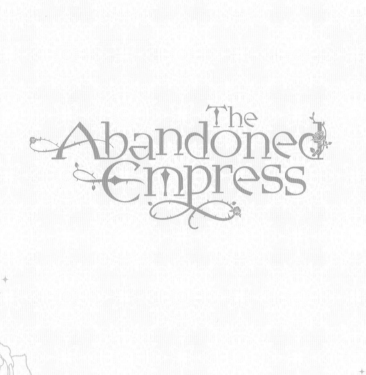

PER MY REQUEST, SIR SEYMORE GUIDED ME IN MY TRAINING IN HIS SPARE MOMENTS.

WATCH YOUR STANCE, MY LADY!

IT WAS NOTHING BEYOND BASIC SWORDSMANSHIP EXERCISES, BUT IT WAS MORE THAN SUFFICIENT TO OVERCOME MY SLUMP.

LET'S CONCLUDE FOR THE DAY. EXCELLENT EFFORT, MY LADY.

THANK YOU AGAIN FOR TODAY, SIR SEYMORE.

YOU'VE BEEN IMPROVING BY LEAPS AND BOUNDS.

IN TRUTH, THERE'S LITTLE FOR ME TO DO.

THE BLOODLINE OF HOUSE MONIQUE LIVES UP TO ITS GLORIOUS REPUTATION, AS EXPECTED.

BUT MY STAGNATION WASN'T LIFTED BY MY ABILITIES ALONE.

OH, I'M JUST A GUARDSMAN...

NO NEED FOR THAT. JOIN ME, PLEASE.

HIS COMING REALLY HAS BEEN A BLESSING.

SIR SEYMORE? IS SOMETHING THE MATTER?

SOMEONE IS APPROACHING.

WHAT? THIS IS THE MANSION'S COURTYARD GARDEN, THOUGH...!

STAND BACK, MY LADY!

RUSTLE

STEP STEP

?!

WHO GOES THERE? SHOW YOURSELF!

CLACK

...A KNIGHT OF THE IMPERIAL GUARD?

WHAT'S A KNIGHT SWORN TO PROTECT THE IMPERIAL FAMILY DOING HERE?

I KNOW THAT VOICE...!

042

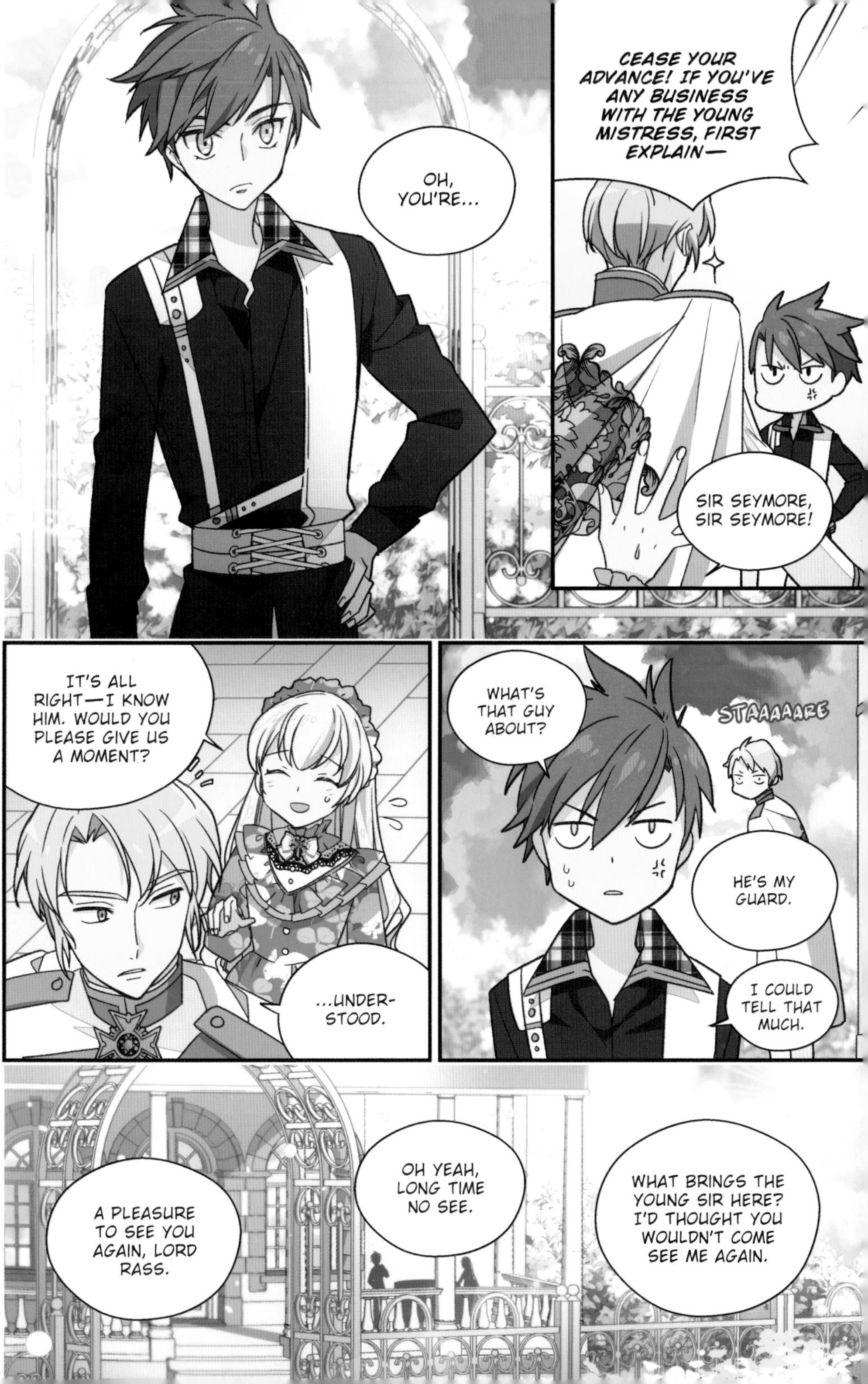
OH, YOU'RE...
CEASE YOUR ADVANCE! IF YOU'VE ANY BUSINESS WITH THE YOUNG MISTRESS, FIRST EXPLAIN—
SIR SEYMORE, SIR SEYMORE!
IT'S ALL RIGHT—I KNOW HIM. WOULD YOU PLEASE GIVE US A MOMENT?
...UNDER-STOOD.
WHAT'S THAT GUY ABOUT?
STAAAAARE
HE'S MY GUARD.
I COULD TELL THAT MUCH.
A PLEASURE TO SEE YOU AGAIN, LORD RASS.
OH YEAH, LONG TIME NO SEE.
WHAT BRINGS THE YOUNG SIR HERE? I'D THOUGHT YOU WOULDN'T COME SEE ME AGAIN.

TELL ME ABOUT IT. I'VE GOT NO CLUE WHY I'M BACK.

...BUT WELL...

...SHE'S LOOKING A LOT BETTER NOW.

PERHAPS THERE'S SOMETHING YOU WISHED TO SAY TO ME?

EH?!

THE MORE I THINK ABOUT IT, THE MORE I COULDN'T JUST LET THAT STAND!

YEAH! OI, YOU!

?!

044

......

...EXCUSE ME?

YOU BUTTED IN LAST TIME AND TOLD ME TO THINK OF MY FAMILY'S HONOR AND ACT LIKE A PROPER NOBLE.

BUT WASN'T IT YOU WHO SPOKE RASHLY TO ME— A GUEST—AND KICKED ME OUT WITH NO RESPECT FOR DIGNITY, YEAH?

EVEN IF WE ARE IN THE SAME FACTION...

...WITH MANNERS AND COMMENTS LIKE THOSE, YOU COULD SPARK A FEUD BETWEEN OUR HOUSES!

SO? GOT ANYTHING TO SAY TO THAT?!

HE CAME TO SAY THIS...?

...INDEED, THE YOUNG SIR MAKES A FINE POINT.

I SHOWED IMPERTINENCE THAT DAY.

PLEASE ACCEPT MY DEEPEST APOLOGIES, LORD RASS.

...MRGH, WHAT?

WHY'RE YOU APOLOGIZING SO EASILY...?

I THOUGHT YOU'D YELL AT ME...

DOES THE YOUNG LORD IMAGINE THE ACT OF APOLOGIZING WOULD INVITE DISREPUTE, THEN?

YEAH, OF COURSE! LOWERING YOUR HEAD TO ANOTHER PERSON—!

WHAT OF IT?

REFUSING TO APOLOGIZE WHEN ONE HAS DONE WRONG...

FAILING TO EXPRESS THANKS WHEN ONE HAS BEEN BLESSED...

LAPSES IN ETIQUETTE SUCH AS THESE ARE THE VERY SIGNS THAT SHOW ONE IS OF ILL REPUTE, DON'T YOU AGREE, YOUNG SIR?

W-WELL, I MEAN...

...THE YOUNG LORD'S RATHER CASUAL ATTITUDE IN SPEAKING WITH AND ADDRESSING ME THUS FAR...

...IS ENOUGH TO SPARK A FEUD BETWEEN OUR HOUSES.

AND SIR IS SURELY WELL AWARE...

ACK!

ER, THAT'S BECAUSE THAT'S...!

S-SORRY— I MEAN, MY APOLOGIES, ESTEEMED YOUNG LADY...

AND I ACCEPT YOUR APOLOGY, YOUNG SIR.

SO, WHAT BUSINESS WAS IT THAT BROUGHT THE YOUNG SIR?

YEAH, I WAS GONNA HELP YOU—WAIT, ER, I'D COME TO THE AID OF HER YOUNG LADY-SHIP...

DID SIR COME TO DISCUSS COURTESY, PERHAPS?

HUH??? WHY DID I COME HERE AGAIN?!

NO, I— NO, THIS YOUNG SIR...

SOD IT ALL—THIS ISN'T WHAT I PLANNED!!

UGH, I GIVE UP! THIS IS JUST HOW I AM! I'M GONNA TALK HOW I WANT TO!

IF YOU DON'T LIKE IT, MAKE A FORMAL COMPLAINT!

UNDERSTOOD. SHALL I SPEAK WITH HIS LORDSHIP THE DUKE?

HRK...! YOU'D REALLY DO THAT?!

GOOD, GREAT. DO IT. GO AHEAD.

URK!

HECK, I'LL JUST GO AHEAD AND DIE.

...WOULD YOU REALLY TELL ON ME LIKE THAT?

......

...MPH.

HUH?

PFFT.

SOUNDS LIKE A BALLOON LOSING AIR...

HEEE...

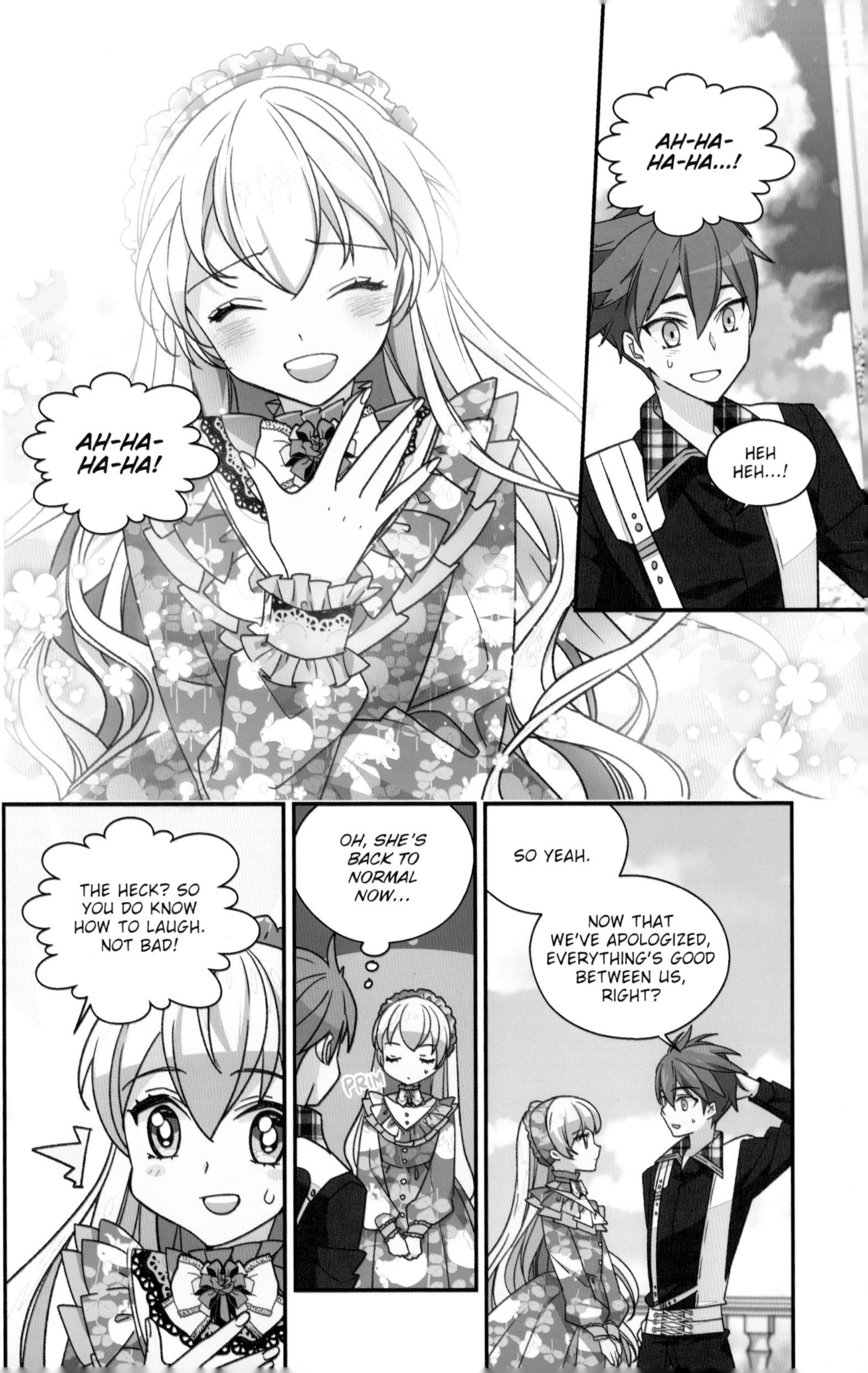
AH-HA-HA-HA!
AH-HA-HA-HA...!
HEH HEH...!
THE HECK? SO YOU DO KNOW HOW TO LAUGH. NOT BAD!
OH, SHE'S BACK TO NORMAL NOW...
PRIM
SO YEAH.
NOW THAT WE'VE APOLOGIZED, EVERYTHING'S GOOD BETWEEN US, RIGHT?

AND WHAT IF IT IS?

THAT MEANS YOU CAN COME OVER TO MY HOUSE AGAIN!

I'VE NO NEED TO GO TO THE YOUNG LORD'S ESTATE NOW.

WHAT? WHY? ARE YOU STILL MAD?!

HEH... LOOK AT THAT FACE.

NO, NOT THAT.

IT'S SIMPLY THAT SIR SEYMORE OVER THERE IS TEACHING ME.

WHA...? THE KNIGHT FROM THE IMPERIAL GUARD? SPEAKING OF...

I WAS WONDERING ABOUT THAT.

WHAT'S AN IMPERIAL KNIGHT DOING HERE?

IT'S NOT LIKE YOU'RE A MEMBER OF THE IMPERIAL HOUSEHOLD, YEAH?

...I'M STILL EXPECTED TO JOIN THE IMPERIAL FAMILY IN THE FUTURE.

HUH?

...IN ANY EVENT, HAVING COME ALL THIS WAY, DO JOIN US FOR A CUP OF TEA, GOOD SIR.

LINA, ANOTHER TEACUP, IF YOU WOULD.

YES, MISS.

IT'S LIKE I CAN SEE THE GEARS TURNING IN HIS HEAD.

I TOLD HIM I WOULDN'T MARRY INTO THE IMPERIAL HOUSE, YET HERE I AM POSTED WITH A GUARD, SO HE MIGHT THINK IT STRANGE.

HMMM...

PLEASE DON'T LET ANYTHING CARELESSLY SLIP IN FRONT OF THE GUARDSMEN...

WELL, WHATEVER, SOUNDS GOOD.

BUT I ALSO HAVE MY ORDERS FROM FATHER, SO NO WAY I CAN JUST LEAVE YOU TO IT!

WHUMP

SO HOW ABOUT THIS?

YOU CAN KEEP GETTING HELP FROM THAT KNIGHT!

AND I'LL JUST COME VISIT YOU!

PARDON?

THE YOUNG SIR WILL COME HERE?

YEAH, EXACTLY! IT'LL BE KILLING TWO BIRDS WITH ONE STONE!

'COS THEN I CAN FINALLY SEE AN IMPERIAL KNIGHT IN ACTION!

IF I CAN ALSO LEARN A THING OR TWO WHILE WE'RE AT IT, ALL THE BETTER!

JUST A MOMENT NOW, LORD RASS. DECIDING SUCH A MATTER SO RASHLY—

IT'LL BE FINE!

MAKING THE TRIP HERE IS NOTHING TO ME!

BUT I'M NOT FINE WITH IT...

PAT

WONDER WHAT THEY'RE TALKING ABOUT...

OKAY, THEN THAT'S THAT!

HOW COMPLETELY OBSTINATE...

I'LL BE IN YOUR HANDS!

AND SO, JUST LIKE THAT—

SINCE WE'RE ALL HERE, LET'S HIT THE TRAINING GROUND AND GET TO IT!

I ENDED UP TRAINING TWICE IN ONE DAY.

WHOA, JUST WHAT I'D EXPECT OF A KNIGHT OF THE IMPERIAL GUARD!

THAT SKILL, THOSE MOVES...!

HM, YEAH. FIRST, PUSH AWAY THE OPPONENT'S WEAPON WITH THE BACK OF THE SWORD...

I'M TELLING YOU, COMING HERE WAS A GREAT CHOICE.

I MEAN, YOU'RE NOT AS GOOD AS THE FIRST ORDER, BUT STILL!

HERE'S YOUR DRINK, YOUNG SIR.

AH, THANKS A BUNCH. I WAS STARTING TO GET A LITTLE PARCHED.

EXCELL—

GULP

UM, THAT'S STILL HOT, THOUGH...

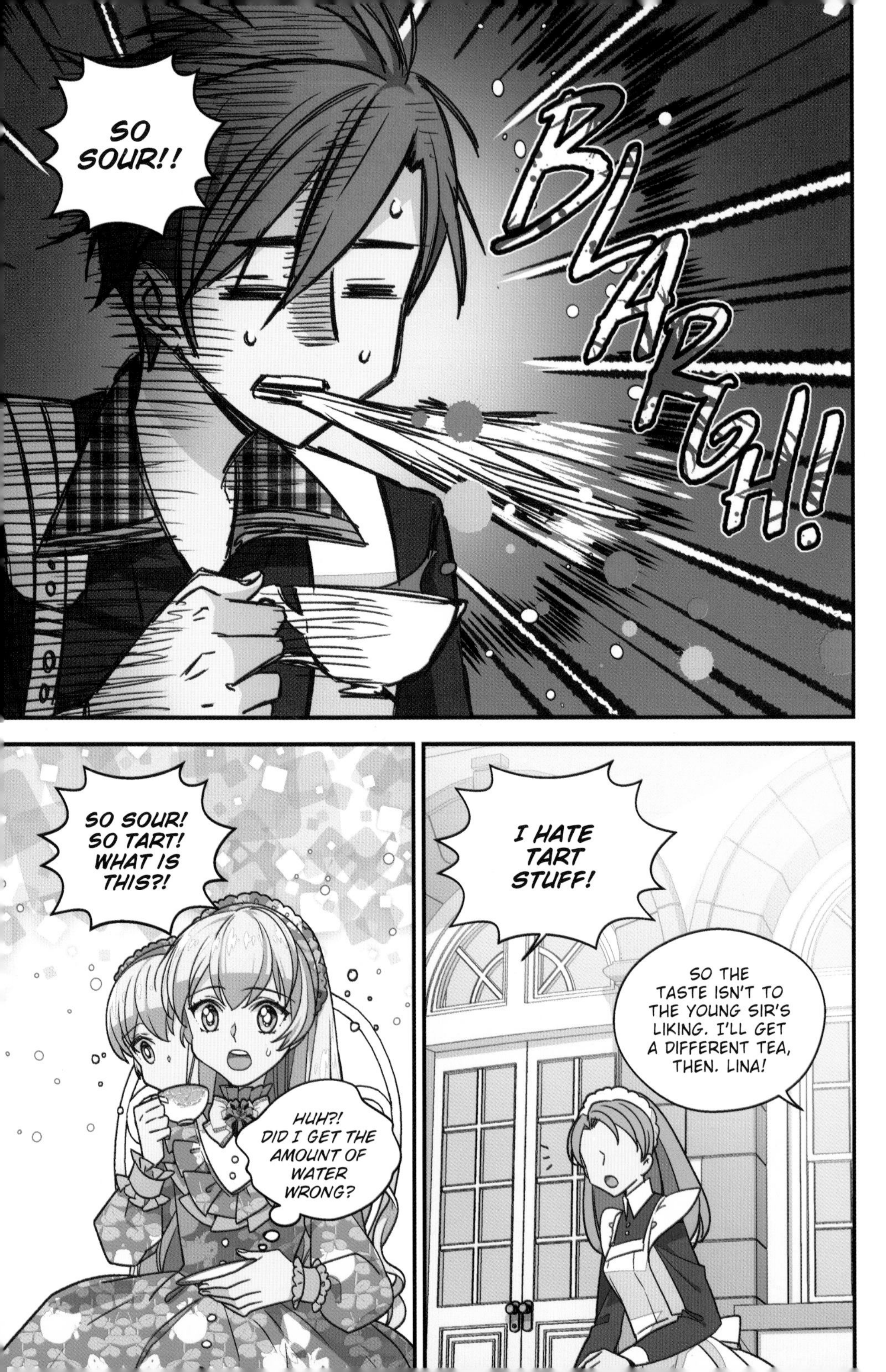
SO SOUR!!
BLARGH!!
SO SOUR! SO TART! WHAT IS THIS?!
HUH?! DID I GET THE AMOUNT OF WATER WRONG?
I HATE TART STUFF!
SO THE TASTE ISN'T TO THE YOUNG SIR'S LIKING. I'LL GET A DIFFERENT TEA, THEN. LINA!

THE COLOR WAS NICE, BUT WHAT A WEIRD TASTE!

AND IT GAVE MY TONGUE A FUNNY FEELING.

YOU SURE IT HASN'T SPOILED OR SOMETHING? OH...

CURRENTLY DRINKING THE SAME TEA WITHOUT ISSUE

THAT'S JUST THE FLAVOR OF THIS PARTICULAR TEA...

IT'S HIBISCUS...

WHAT, REALLY?! AND YOU LIKE IT?!

I DO INDEED.

ARE YOU TWO HARD OF TASTING OR SOMETHING?!!

I MEAN, I KNEW AS MUCH WHEN WE FIRST MET, BUT YOU REALLY HAVE SOME PECULIAR TASTES!

THEN BY ALL MEANS, DON'T DRINK IT!!

?!

SWIPE

SINCE I HAVE SUCH PECULIAR TASTES...

...EVEN IF I SHOULD SERVE THE YOUNG LORD A DIFFERENT TEA, IT WOULDN'T SUIT HIS MOST CIVILIZED PALATE!

HUH...?

EH?! O-OI!!

HMPH!

CLATTER

SERIOUSLY? NOT LIKE I SAID ANYTHING WRONG... IT TASTED TART, SO I SAID IT WAS TART. THAT'S ALL.

ISN'T THAT RIGHT, SIR SEYMORE?

HA-HA...

IT IS HARD TO SAY, LORD RASS. I, FOR ONE, HAVEN'T ANY SPECIAL AFFINITY FOR TEA, BUT...

...AS IT WAS TEA MADE BY THE YOUNG LADY HERSELF, THAT ALONE IS QUITE THE HONOR FOR ME.

SHE'S SAID THAT SHE QUITE ENJOYS THE ART OF BREWING TEA.

......

...WHAT?

THE LADY. HER. SELF.

......

ER... UM...

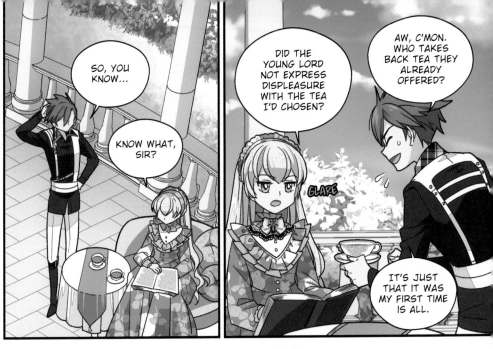

SO, YOU KNOW...

KNOW WHAT, SIR?

DID THE YOUNG LORD NOT EXPRESS DISPLEASURE WITH THE TEA I'D CHOSEN?

AW, C'MON. WHO TAKES BACK TEA THEY ALREADY OFFERED?

IT'S JUST THAT IT WAS MY FIRST TIME IS ALL.

CLARE

URP

NGH...IT'S LIKE THE TARTEST THING TO EVER TART...

IT'S NOT LIKE I CAN'T DRINK IT! GYAH-HA-HA-HA!

YEAH, THAT'S RIGHT!

......

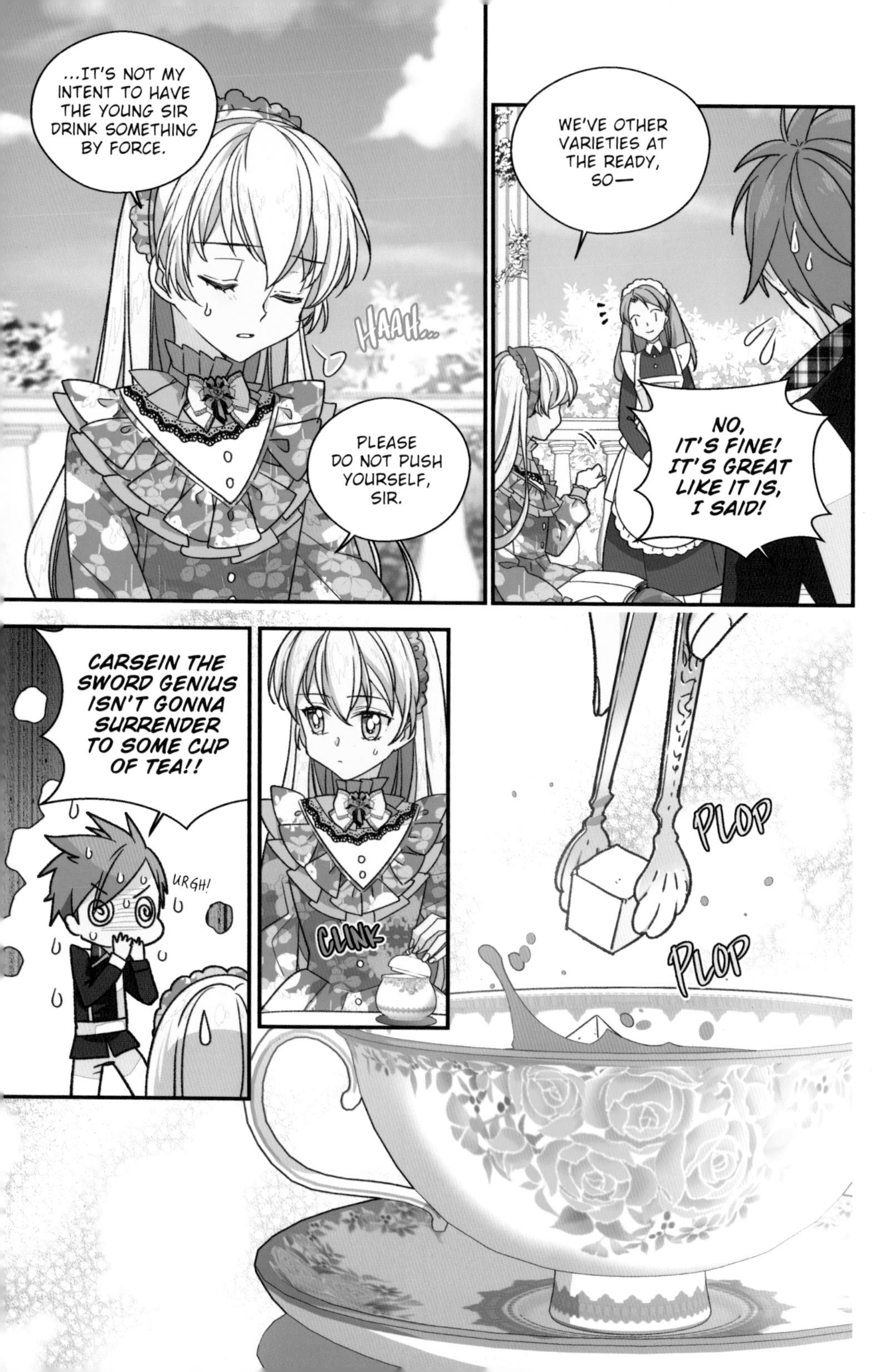
...IT'S NOT MY INTENT TO HAVE THE YOUNG SIR DRINK SOMETHING BY FORCE.
HAAAH...
PLEASE DO NOT PUSH YOURSELF, SIR.
WE'VE OTHER VARIETIES AT THE READY, SO—
NO, IT'S FINE! IT'S GREAT LIKE IT IS, I SAID!
CARSEIN THE SWORD GENIUS ISN'T GONNA SURRENDER TO SOME CUP OF TEA!!
URGH!
CLINK
PLOP
PLOP

HERE YOU ARE.

PLEASE TRY IT NOW.

SLURP...

SLURP

SLURP

SLURP

SLURP

...HM?!

HEY, THAT'S A LOT BETTER.

IS THAT RIGHT, NOW?

LORD RASS—

HE'S QUITE PECULIAR.

HE SPEAKS WITHOUT ANY ARTIFICE, SIMPLY REVEALING WHAT HE FEELS.

IT HAS A WAY OF DRAWING ME IN AND CAUSING ME TO ACT IN WAYS I NEVER HAVE BEFORE.

THAT'S THE FIRST TIME I'VE EVER BURST INTO LAUGHTER THAT HAD ME GRIPPING MY STOMACH.

PERHAPS SUCH A THING...

...IS NOT SO BAD.

THOUGH MY ONCE-QUIET DAYS ARE GETTING NOISY...

JUST WHAT...

...ARE YOU GETTING AT?

ONLY TO SAY THAT WE REGARD YOUR HIGHNESS AS MOST OUTSTANDING...

IT IS MERELY THAT WE RECENTLY ENCOUNTERED IN PASSING THE YOUNG DAUGHTER OF HOUSE MONIQUE...

...AND THERE ARE THOSE EVEN IN THE PALACE OF THE KINGDOM OF LISA WHO ADMIRE HIS HIGHNESS.

HA-HA!

...AND SAW SHE IS STILL MUCH TOO YOUNG TO SUPPLY YOUR HIGHNESS WITH HIS DUE AID.

......

W-WELL ...!

OF COURSE, AS THE PROPHESIED CHILD...

...SHE CARRIED HERSELF WITH SUCH AN ELEGANCE AS WOULD BEFIT A FUTURE EMPRESS OF THE NATION!

...AND?

WHAT DOES MY FIANCÉE'S AGE HAVE TO DO WITH THE TWO OF YOU?

WE COULD DO NAUGHT BUT BOW OUR HEADS BEFORE HER!

AHEM...

AS AN EMPRESS, SHE WILL HAVE MANY BURDENSOME RESPONSIBILITIES...

...AND TO LESSEN THE LOAD, HIS HIGHNESS SURELY NEEDS SOMEONE TO AID HIM.

OUR PRINCESSES OF THE KINGDOM OF LISA HAVE DEVOTED THEIR VERY LIVES TO LEARNING HOW BETTER THEY COULD BE OF HELP TO THE EMPIRE AND THE IMPERIAL HOUSEHOLD!

WE DO HOPE HIS HIGHNESS WILL GIVE HIS KIND CONSIDERATION TO THIS POINT ABOUT—

...AS THE IMPERIAL CONSORT, CORRECT?

...IN OTHER WORDS...

...SOMETHING LIKE THAT, YES, TO PUT IT PLAINLY.

THIS IS ONLY OUT OF A SINCERE WISH TO SOON SEE THE IMPERIAL LINE OF SUCCESSION SAFELY ESTABLISHED, HIGHNESS.

TRULY?

IT SEEMS INDEED THAT THE LISA KINGDOM IS EXCEPTIONALLY LOYAL TO THE EMPIRE.

TO THE POINT WHERE, WHILE HIS MAJESTY MY FATHER IS YET HALE AND HEARTY...

...YOU'VE ELECTED TO COME TO ME, STILL AN UNMARRIED MAN...

...TO PROFESS YOUR FEARS REGARDING THE HEIR OF THE IMPERIAL FAMILY.

EXCEPTIONAL IS SUCH GENUINE COURAGE.

SO EXCEPTIONAL, IN FACT, IT EVEN MERITS INFORMING ALL THE OTHER OFFICIALS THAT THEY OUGHT TO FOLLOW SUIT.

SHIVER

......

...HMM.

I SHALL NOTE WELL THE LISA KINGDOM'S INTENTIONS.

I SUPPOSE THIS EXPLAINS WHAT THEY WERE AIMING FOR, SENDING SO MANY DELEGATIONS.

WE ARE HONORED GREATLY, YOUR HIGHNESS.

AND ALL THOSE TRIBUTES TOO...

TSK!

THEY CAME TO SPEAK DIRECTLY WITH ME BECAUSE THEY KNOW HIS MAJESTY WOULD'VE HEARD NONE OF IT.

...IMPERIAL CONSORT, HUH?

AS WITH THE TITLE OF EMPRESS ITSELF, ONLY ONE INDIVIDUAL IS MEANT TO HOLD IT...

...AND IS MEANT TO SERVE AS A FACILITATOR TO THE EMPRESS AND TO ASSUME HER FUNCTIONS IN EXTRAORDINARY CIRCUMSTANCES.

AS THAT CHILD'S STILL YOUNG...

...IF THE IMPERIAL CONSORT IS WITH CHILD FIRST, THAT BABY WOULD HAVE A LEGITIMATE CLAIM TO THE THRONE.

...THAT'S THEIR SCHEME.

THAT'S WHY THEY WANT TO POSITION ONE OF THEIR OWN PRINCESSES IN THAT SECOND SEAT.

ONE CAN'T KNOW FOR SURE THAT THERE ISN'T A PRINCESS OF SOME KINGDOM WHO TRULY DOES ADMIRE HIS HIGHNESS, NO?

STOP TALKING NONSENSE.

STILL YOUNG INDEED.

AND YET UNABLE EVEN TO SAY THAT SHE'S UNWELL AND NEEDS TO REST.

...SHOULD I GO...

......

YES?

?

......

NEVER MIND.

SINCE THE COURT PHYSICIAN WENT TO SEE HER...

...SHE SHOULD BE BACK ON HER FEET NOW.

*THAT THOUGHT
WAS QUITE
UNNECESSARY.*

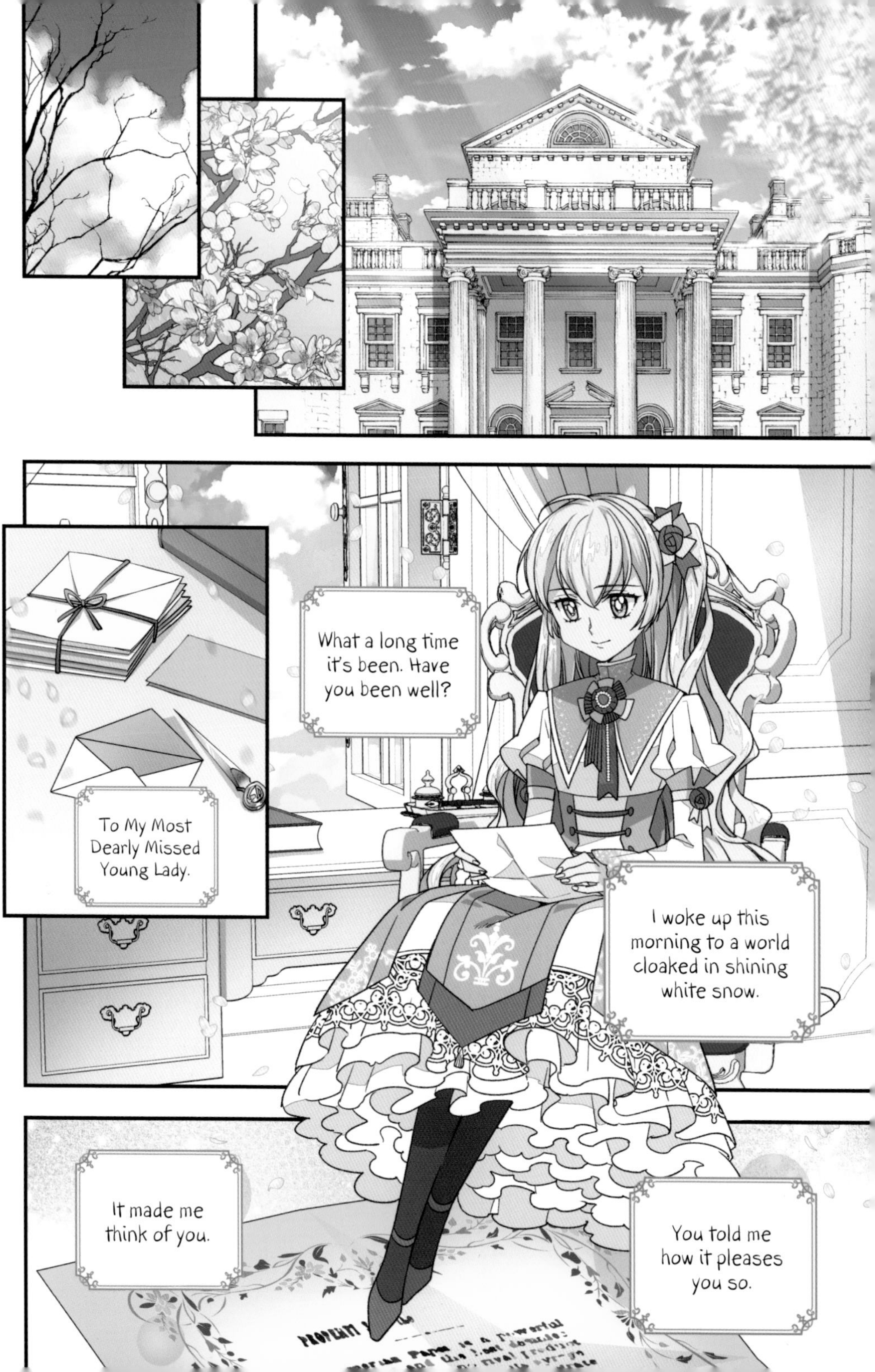
To My Most Dearly Missed Young Lady.
What a long time it's been. Have you been well?
I woke up this morning to a world cloaked in shining white snow.
It made me think of you.
You told me how it pleases you so.

Do you recall the mischief from last winter?

Sir Ecks and Sir Mor started the snowball fight, remember?

"Something as sweet, warm, and white as snow."

Sir Lieg joined in after being struck in passing...

...and man by man, it escalated into an outright war.

EEEEK!
MILADY!!

Eventually, a
stray snowball hit
you, and the real
chaos ensued.

ARISTIA!!

WHUD!

You caught
such a terrible
cold in the end.

Did you
know?

I was terrified
to be on the
training field
that day.

Yet I'll bet you're laughing, reading this.

WELL, YOU'VE GOT ME THERE.

His Lordship was positively merciless. Truly, I thought at least one person would die.

And take care not to overtax yourself by training alone in snowy fields.

And so, Aristia, do dress warmly when venturing out.

Come spring, a special gift shall arrive for you.

Do look out for it, my lady.

A GIFT?

P.S. It's sweet, warm, and white, just as you like!

......

OH, ALLENDIS. REALLY...

TO THINK HOW BUSY HE MUST BE, AND YET HE REMEMBERS SUCH THINGS.

...HE COULDN'T POSSIBLY HAVE MADE HIS WHITE CHOCOLATE FROM SO FAR AWAY, COULD HE?

GIFTS... OH WAIT!

LINA!

BRING ME MY CRAFTING SUPPLIES!

WHATEVER FOR, YOUNG MISS?

I'M GOING TO MAKE BOOKMARKS.

OH, AND BRING ALONG THE SILVER TASSELS LEFT OVER FROM LAST YEAR AS WELL!

HEY! YOU'RE IN HIGH SPIRITS TODAY, HUH?

GOOD MORNING, LORD RASS!

WHATCHA MAKING?

BOOKMARKS AND SWORD POMMEL DECORATIONS.

AND WHO'RE THEY FOR?

THEY'RE FOR THOSE IN THE SECOND ORDER OF KNIGHTS, OFF FAR AFIELD...

...AND FOR A TREASURED FRIEND.

WHAT WITH THEIR LEAVING SO ABRUPTLY, I WASN'T ABLE TO GIVE THEM ANYTHING.

SO I'M GOING TO PUT THESE TOGETHER AND PRAY FOR THEIR SAFE RETURN WHILST I WAIT.

HMM... A TREASURED FRIEND, YOU SAY.

081

HOW ABOUT MINE?

COME AGAIN?

WHAT'RE YOU GONNA MAKE FOR ME?

AND WHY OUGHT I TO MAKE THE YOUNG SIR A PRESENT?

WHY NOT?! C'MON, WE TRAIN TOGETHER EVERY DAY!

SO?

WE'RE NOT ON GIFT-GIVING TERMS, CORRECT?

WAIT, WE'RE NOT?!!

I'M JUST GONNA GO OUTSIDE, THEN!

AH, VERY GOOD. I'LL FINISH UP HERE AND BE OUT SHORTLY AS WELL.

GRAAAH!!

DID HE REALLY WANT A BOOKMARK?

?

THANK YOU FOR WAITING, LORD RASS!

LET US START TODAY'S TRAINING!

HWO OSH

......?

NOBODY'S HERE?

HAVE THEY GONE OFF SOMEWHERE?

I SUPPOSE I SHOULD JUST START WITH RUNNING.

flutter

MY, WHAT
NICE
WEATHER.

I FEEL QUITE
INVIGORATED
TODAY.

IT MIGHT BE
FORESHADOWING
GOOD FORTUNE.

HM?

WHOOSH

......?

IT FEELS AS THOUGH SOMEONE'S OVER THERE.

AM I JUST IMAGINING THINGS? OR PERHAPS...

RUSTLE

TA TMP TMP TMP

I KNEW IT— IT MUST BE LORD RASS.

WHO

MP

WAIT...!

J-JUST A MINUTE, NOW, LORD—!

WHAT DO YOU THINK YOU'RE DO-ING ALL OF A SUDD—

ARISTIA.

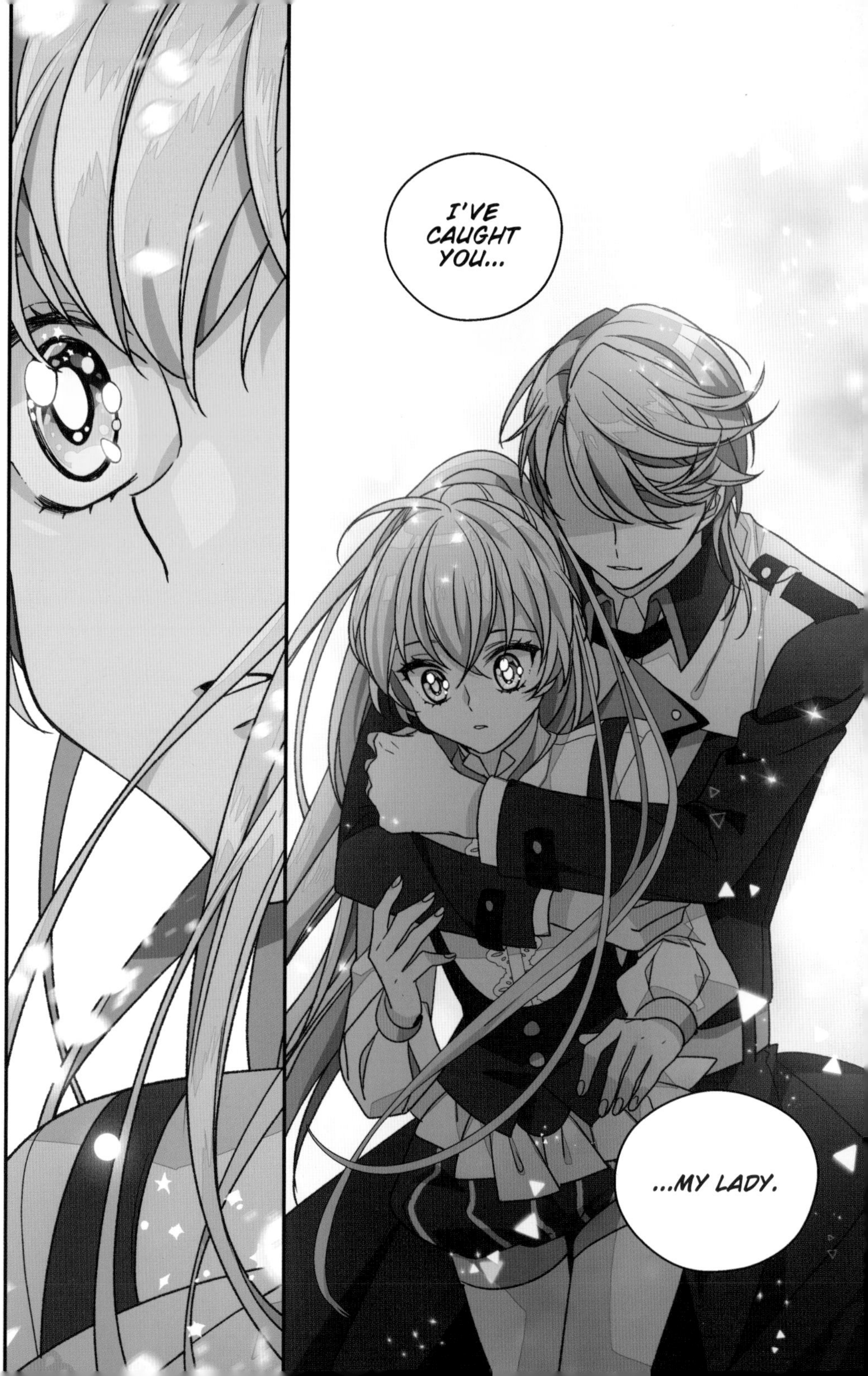
I'VE CAUGHT YOU...
...MY LADY.

JUST LIKE THE DELICATE NEW BLOOMS OF SPRING...

...THE VOICE I HAD LONG YEARNED FOR CAREFULLY REACHED MY EARS.

A...

IT CAN'T...!

ALLENDIS...?

IT'S BEEN FAR TOO LONG, ARISTIA.

ALLENDIS, I'VE MISSED YOU!

HA-HA-HA!

HUG♡

AS I HAVE YOU, MY LADY!

SQUEEZE

AH...
IT'S LIKE
I'M ALIVE AT
LAST AGAIN!

THAT
FAMILIAR
TOUCH THAT
USED TO
STROKE MY
HEAD...

I'M BACK IN
THAT WONDERFUL
EMBRACE.

⁇⁉❗

WHAT IN THE
WORLD AM I
LOOKING AT?!?!!

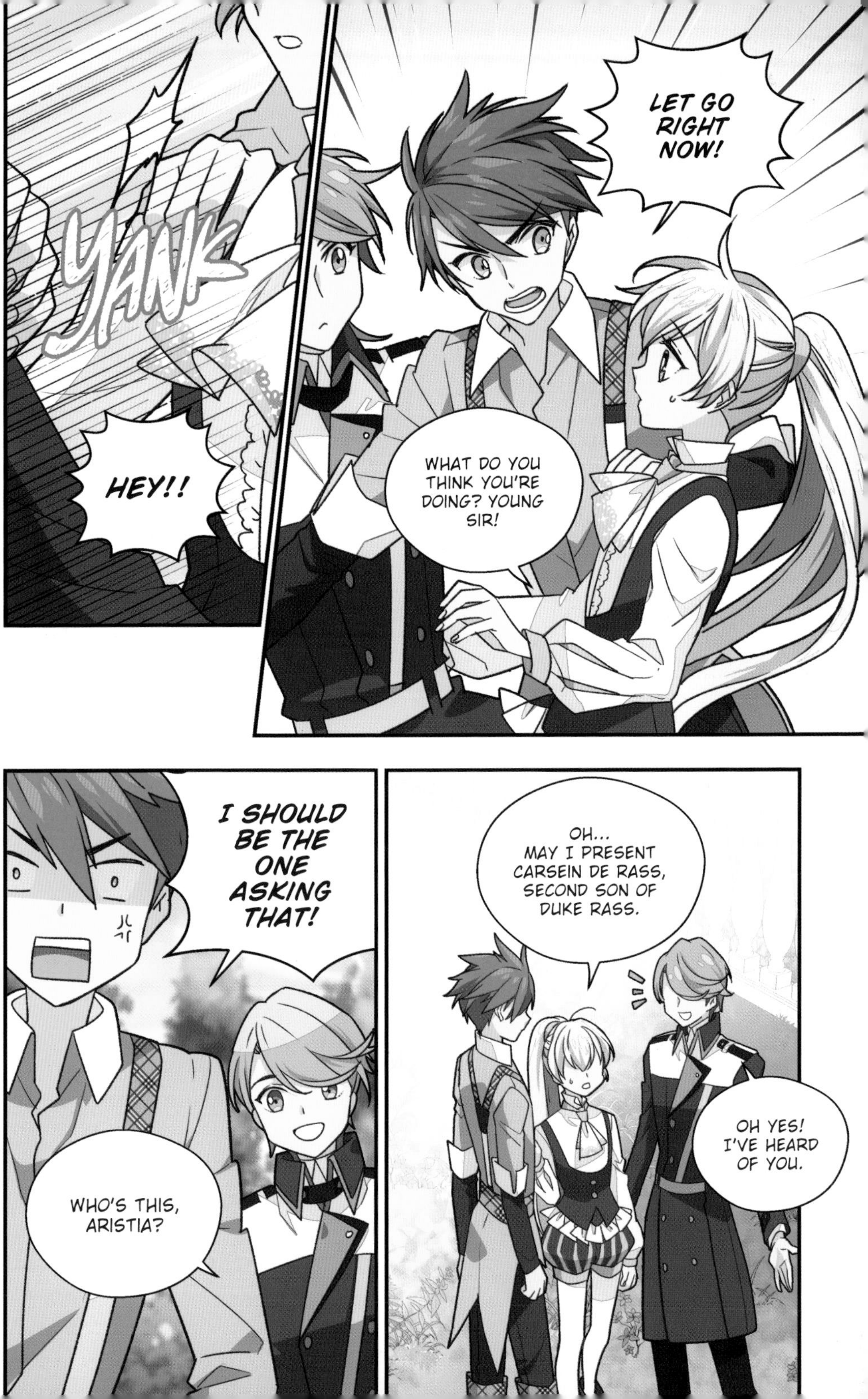
YANK
HEY!!
LET GO RIGHT NOW!
WHAT DO YOU THINK YOU'RE DOING? YOUNG SIR!
I SHOULD BE THE ONE ASKING THAT!
WHO'S THIS, ARISTIA?
OH... MAY I PRESENT CARSEIN DE RASS, SECOND SON OF DUKE RASS.
OH YES! I'VE HEARD OF YOU.

I AM ALLENDIS DE VERITA.

I SEE YOU'VE SERVED AS A FRIEND TO ARISTIA WHILE I'VE BEEN AWAY.

A PLEASURE AND HONOR, SIR.

......

OI, YOU.

I DIDN'T THINK YOU WERE THE DISCRIMINATING TYPE!

I'M THE SAME AGE AS THIS GUY! WHY D'YOU CALL ME "SIR" AND "LORD" BUT CALL HIM BY HIS NAME?!

AND YOU TALK DIFFERENTLY TO HIM TOO!

WHY'S HE SO ANGRY?

THEN CALL ME BY MY NAME TOO! YOU'VE GOT MY PERMISSION!!

WELL, ALLENDIS AND I AGREED TO CALL EACH OTHER BY NAME.

I THINK I SHAN'T, LORD RASS.

MOREOVER, SIR, DO RETURN A PROPER GREETING FIRST. OR WOULD YOU BE SO DISCOURTEOUS AT A FIRST MEETING?

...TSK!

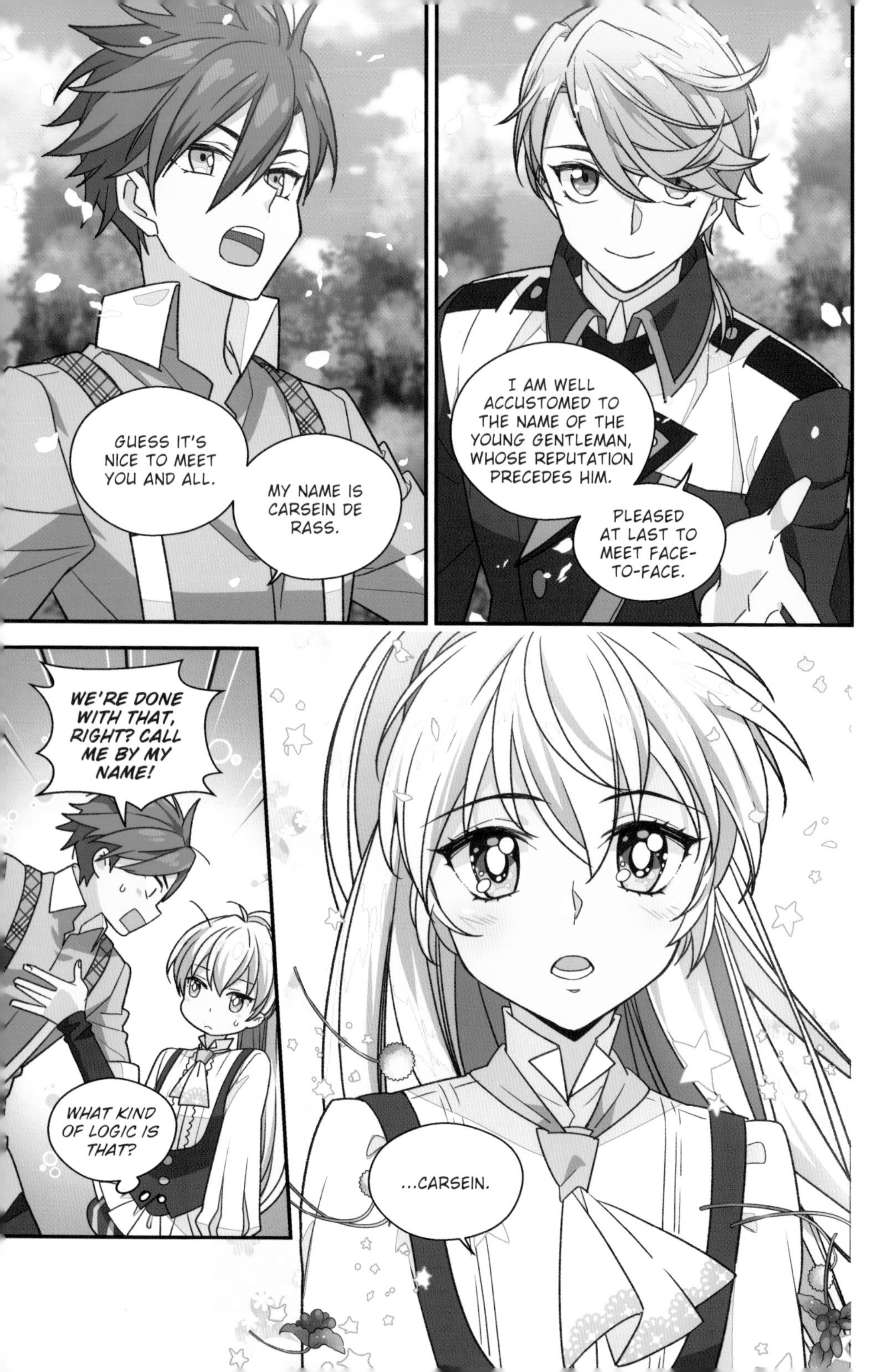
GUESS IT'S NICE TO MEET YOU AND ALL.
MY NAME IS CARSEIN DE RASS.
I AM WELL ACCUSTOMED TO THE NAME OF THE YOUNG GENTLEMAN, WHOSE REPUTATION PRECEDES HIM.
PLEASED AT LAST TO MEET FACE-TO-FACE.
WE'RE DONE WITH THAT, RIGHT? CALL ME BY MY NAME!
WHAT KIND OF LOGIC IS THAT?
...CARSEIN.

YAAAY!

IS THE YOUNG SIR SATISFIED?

URGH...

WHY'RE YOU STILL TALKING ALL FANCY?!

YOU'D ASKED IF I MIGHT CALL YOU BY NAME—NOTHING OF DEFERRING DEFERENCE.

ARGH, THE HECK?! YOU'RE MAKIN' IT SO COMPLICATED!

HEH-HEH!

......

HEE HEE!

I'VE RETURNED AFTER ALL THIS TIME, AND YOU DON'T HAVE A GIFT TO GIVE ME?

HM? WAS THERE SOMETHING YOU WERE HOPING FOR?

THERE IS. AND YOU WOULDN'T MIND GIVING IT TO ME?

OF COURSE I WOULDN'T!

I'LL JUST GIVE HIM HIS BOOKMARK ANOTHER TIME...

YOUR NICKNAME.

ONE'S NICKNAME IS ONLY USED BY FAMILY OR THE MOST INTIMATE OF RELATIONSHIPS...

MY...

...NICK-NAME?

I BELIEVE IT'S RATHER UNCOMMON FOR FRIENDS TO DO SO...?

WHAT TO DO? AS THE CROWN-PRINCESS-TO-BE, I'M WORRIED ABOUT POTENTIAL BACKLASH FROM THE IMPERIAL HOUSE...

BUT TO REFUSE MIGHT HURT ALLENDIS...

WHY'S SHE SO FORMAL WITH ME?!

DON'T WORRY.

I WON'T CALL YOU BY IT IN FRONT OF ANY OTHERS.

HAVE NO FEAR IN THAT REGARD.

STILL BUSY RANTING

ALL RIGHT, THEN. YOU HAVE MY LEAVE.

THANK YOU SO KINDLY, TIA. AND WOULD YOU CALL ME THUSLY?

IT'S THE FIRST TIME I'VE HEARD MY NICKNAME SPOKEN BY ONE OUTSIDE MY FAMILY...

...ALLEN.

HOW I ONCE WISHED TO HEAR THOSE TWO SIMPLE SYLLABLES FROM HIS MOUTH.

WATCHING THOSE TWO TALKING SO SWEETLY TO EACH OTHER BACK THEN...

...I WAS ENDLESSLY ENVIOUS OF JIEUN.

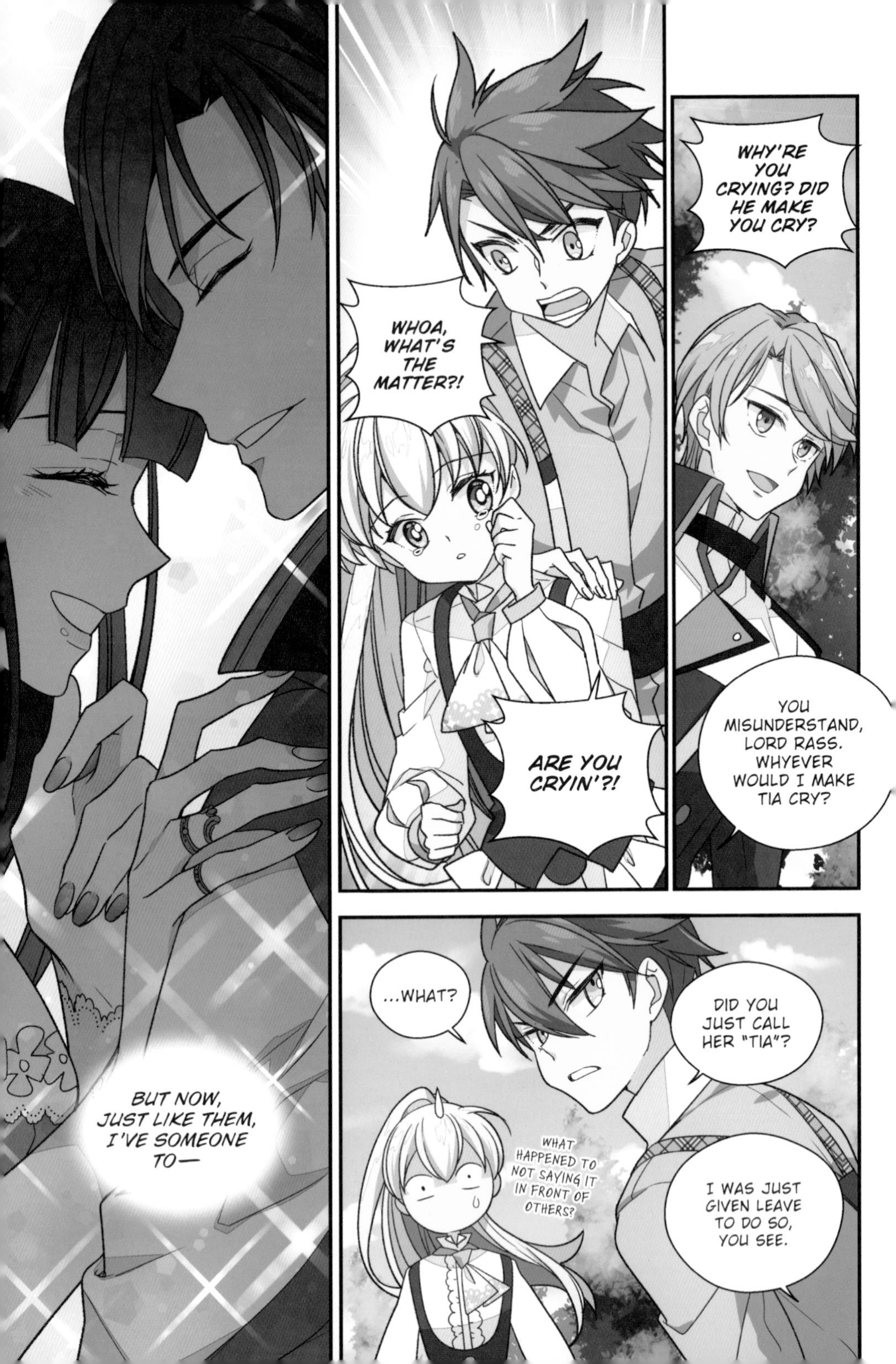

BUT NOW, JUST LIKE THEM, I'VE SOMEONE TO—
WHOA, WHAT'S THE MATTER?!
ARE YOU CRYIN'?!
WHY'RE YOU CRYING? DID HE MAKE YOU CRY?
YOU MISUNDERSTAND, LORD RASS. WHYEVER WOULD I MAKE TIA CRY?
...WHAT?
DID YOU JUST CALL HER "TIA"?
I WAS JUST GIVEN LEAVE TO DO SO, YOU SEE.
WHAT HAPPENED TO NOT SAYING IT IN FRONT OF OTHERS?

KRAAAACKLE

TIA, WOULD YOU GO BACK IN AHEAD OF US?

IT'S JUST, WE'VE A THING OR TWO TO DISCUSS BETWEEN US.

OH, SURE.

WELL THEN, I'LL AWAIT THE BOTH OF YOU IN THE DRAW-ING ROOM.

HA!

ARE THEY GOING TO BE ALL RIGHT?

ALLEN AT LEAST IS QUITE MATURE, SO I CAN LEAVE MATTERS IN HIS HANDS, RIGHT?

LINA!
OH, LINA!

BRING OUT OUR BEST LEMON BALM TEA LEAVES!

TAYLOR, GO ASK THE KITCHEN TO PREPARE SNACKS FOR AFTERNOON TEA QUICKLY!

EVERYONE, THE DRAWING ROOM NEEDS FRESHENING UP—

I KNOW! LIGHT THOSE PERFUMED CANDLES WE JUST GOT!

YES!!

OH MY, YOUNG MISS! ARE YOU REALLY SO EXCITED?

YOU'RE SMILING FROM EAR TO EAR!

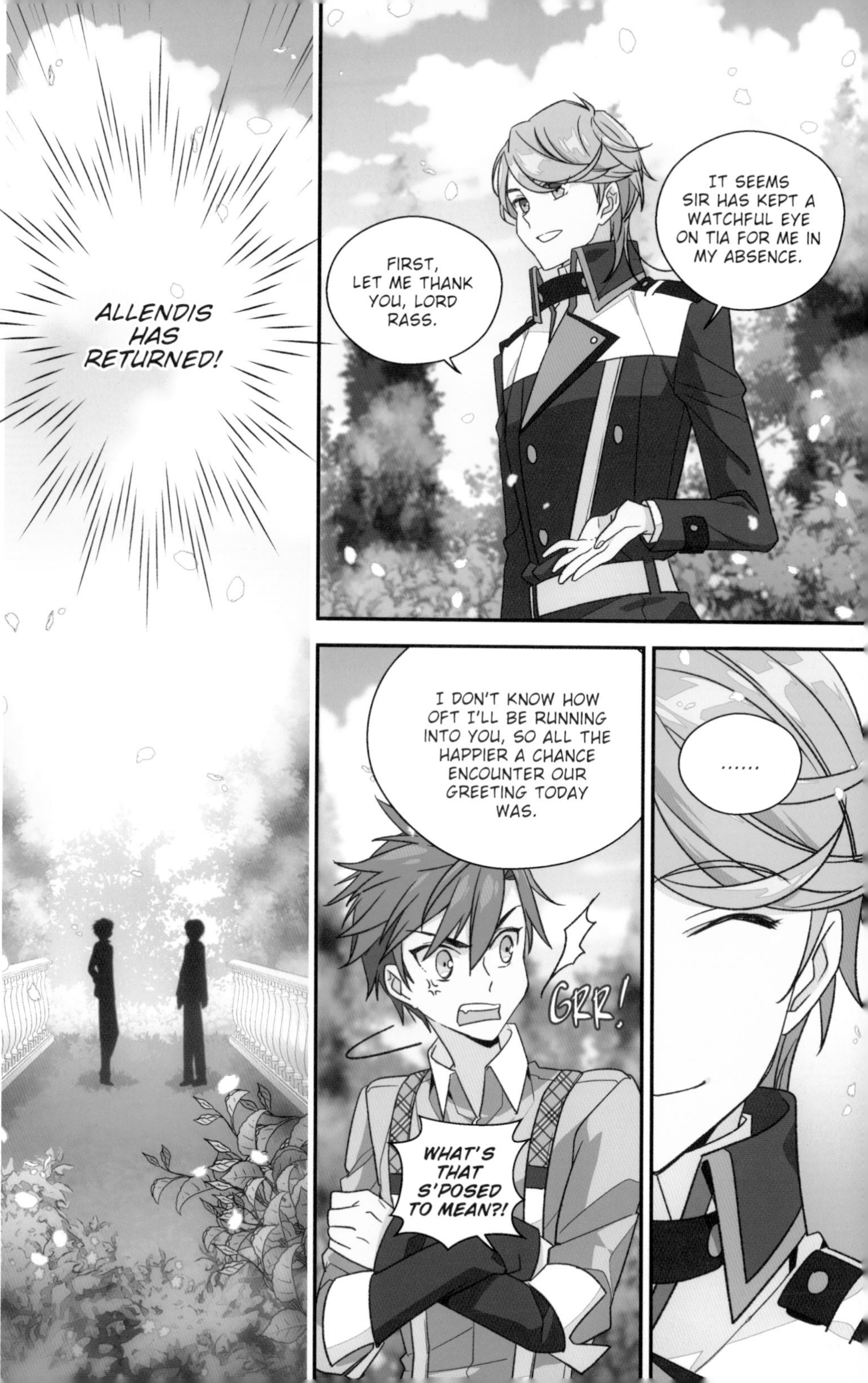
ALLENDIS HAS RETURNED!
FIRST, LET ME THANK YOU, LORD RASS.
IT SEEMS SIR HAS KEPT A WATCHFUL EYE ON TIA FOR ME IN MY ABSENCE.
I DON'T KNOW HOW OFT I'LL BE RUNNING INTO YOU, SO ALL THE HAPPIER A CHANCE ENCOUNTER OUR GREETING TODAY WAS.
......
GRR!
WHAT'S THAT S'POSED TO MEAN?!

HEY, LOOK, I'VE GOT YOU MORE OR LESS FIGURED OUT, SO HOW 'BOUT YOU DROP THE ACT AND SHOW YOUR TRUE COLORS?

...HA.

C'MON, SERIOUSLY?

WHATEVER DOES THE GOOD SIR MEAN?

I MEAN HOW YOU PRETEND TO BE A NICE GUY IN FRONT OF HER—

I SAW RIGHT THROUGH YOU.

......!

YOU SPROUT BASTARD.

HW

OO

SH

...HA!

HEH HEH!!

I SEE.

YOU'RE NOT JUST FRIVOLOUS AND ILL-MANNERED— IT SEEMS YOU MIGHT EVEN BE QUITE PERCEPTIVE.

PERHAPS IT'S YOUR "ANIMAL INSTINCTS"...

...YOU CARROT JERK.

...HA!

SO THAT'S YOUR REAL FACE.

WHAT? SAY THAT AGAIN. CARROT?

YOU CALLED ME A SPROUT, DID YOU NOT?

HONESTLY, WHAT A CHOICE OF INSULT.

I'M MATCHING YOUR LEVEL BY CHOOSING A GARDEN VARIETY OF YOUR HAIR COLOR.

I'D HATE TO HAVE IT SAIL OVER YOUR HEAD, AFTER ALL.

PLUS, CARROTS BEING ROOT VEGETABLES, IT'D MEAN THAT YOU'RE BENEATH ME. WHICH IS FITTING, NO?

YOU—!!

SHO CK

AWAWA!

RUSH

BE CAREFUL
HOW YOU RUN
YOUR MOUTH...!

LIKEWISE—
I SUGGEST YOU
SCRAM.

THE HELL ARE YOU TALKING ABOUT?! AND WHAT IF I DON'T?!

SHE'S MINE. I WON'T HAND HER OVER TO ANYONE ELSE.

HUH?! JUST HOW'S SHE "YOURS"?

SWAT

WHAT DO YOU KNOW ABOUT TIA?

...NGH.

LISTEN UP. THE DAY WE FIRST MET...

...WAS THE THIRD DAY OF THE NINTH MONTH OF YEAR 958 OF THE EMPIRE, 2:43 IN THE AFTERNOON.

SHE WAS WEARING A WHITE KNEE-LENGTH DRESS TRIMMED IN BLUE.

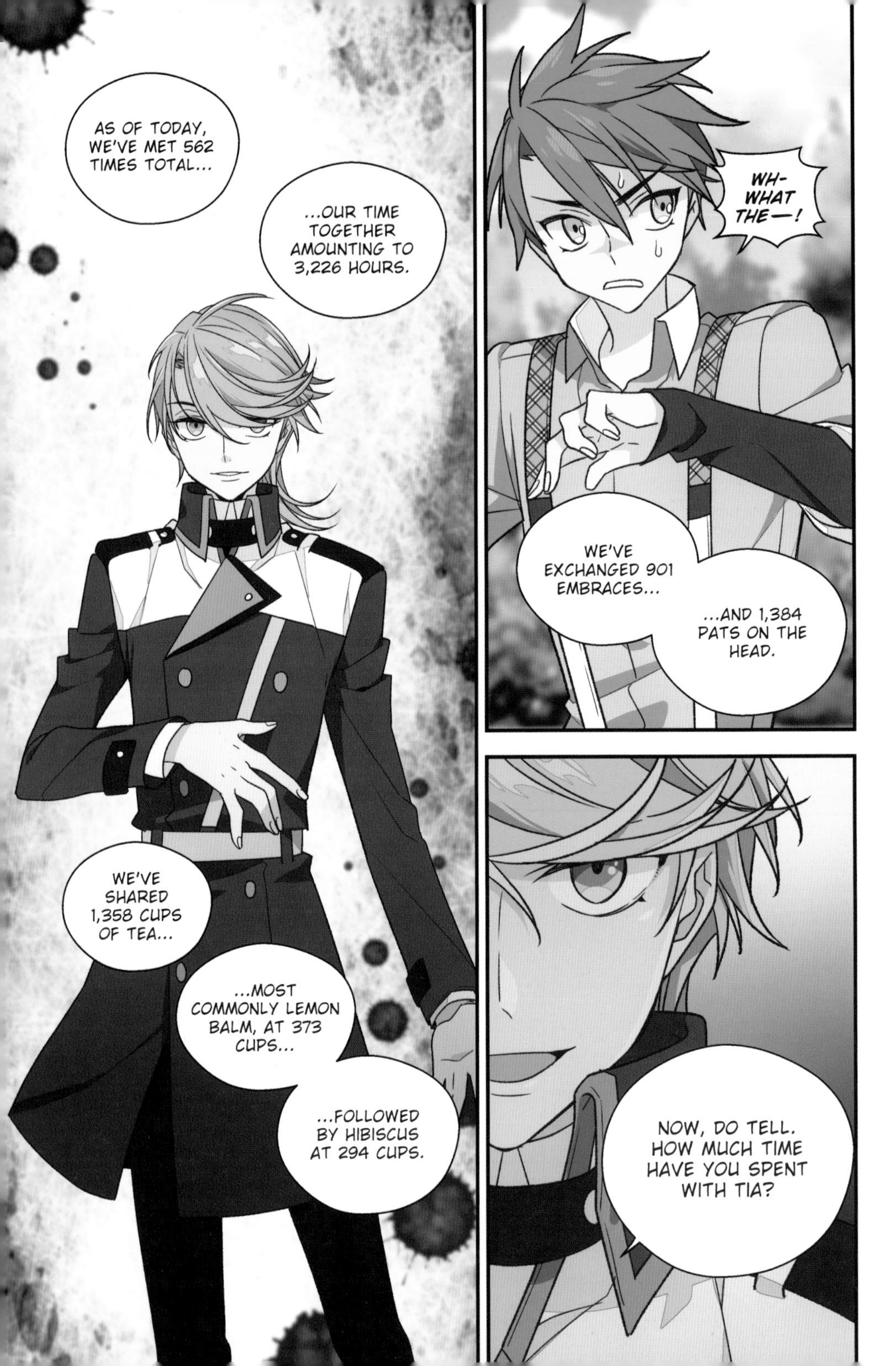
AS OF TODAY, WE'VE MET 562 TIMES TOTAL...
...OUR TIME TOGETHER AMOUNTING TO 3,226 HOURS.
WE'VE SHARED 1,358 CUPS OF TEA...
...MOST COMMONLY LEMON BALM, AT 373 CUPS...
...FOLLOWED BY HIBISCUS AT 294 CUPS.
WH- WHAT THE—!
WE'VE EXCHANGED 901 EMBRACES...
...AND 1,384 PATS ON THE HEAD.
NOW, DO TELL. HOW MUCH TIME HAVE YOU SPENT WITH TIA?

HAVE YOU LOST YOUR MIND?!

YOU'VE BEEN COUNTING ALL THAT STUFF?!

OI, YOU WEED! DOES SHE KNOW YOU'RE BARKING MAD?

DID IT LOOK LIKE SHE DID?

GRAH, WHAT A LUNATIC!!

WHAT IT LOOKS LIKE IS I'D BETTER LET HER KNOW, QUICK!!

HMPH.

YOU FOOL.

WHAT?!

ARE YOU SURE, LINA?

YES, IT'S ALL TRUE! YOUNG LORD VERITA WAS SAYING SOMETHING, AND YOUNG LORD RASS'S FACE WAS ALL MENACING, AND HE GRABBED HIS COLLAR LIKE—!

IT REALLY SEEMED LIKE THEY WERE ABOUT TO EXCHANGE BLOWS!

I HADN'T EXACTLY THOUGHT THE TWO OF THEM WOULD BECOME GOOD FRIENDS RIGHT FROM THE START, BUT...

IT'S CLEAR AS DAY WHAT THIS IS.

IT'S JEALOUSY, PLAIN AND SIMPLE.

WHAT?

THEY EACH KNEW NOTHING OF THE OTHER BEFORE NOW, RIGHT?

SO WHAT ELSE COULD THEY BE FIGHTING OVER BUT THE YOUNG MISS?

OH, LINA, THAT'S NONSENSE.

REALLY, LINA... YOU'VE BEEN READING TOO MANY ROMANCE STORIES LATELY, TO THINK SUCH A THING.

I MIGHT NOT KNOW MUCH ABOUT YOUNG LORD RASS, BUT I'M SURE OF YOUNG LORD VERITA!

HE WAS AWAY AND RETURNED TO FIND A NEW YOUNG GENTLEMAN HERE, SO HE MUST BE VEXED!

I MUST ADMIT, I DO LIKE NOVELS—BUT THE POINT STANDS, YOUNG MISS!

ALLENDIS IS JUST MY FRIEND, THOUGH.

JUST A "FRIEND" WHO PROPOSED MARRIAGE?

THAT'S ONLY BARELY A MEMORY, OF YOUNGER DAYS PASSED.

...IT CERTAINLY COULDN'T BE THE CASE THAT ANY BOY WOULD LIKE ME IN SUCH A WAY.

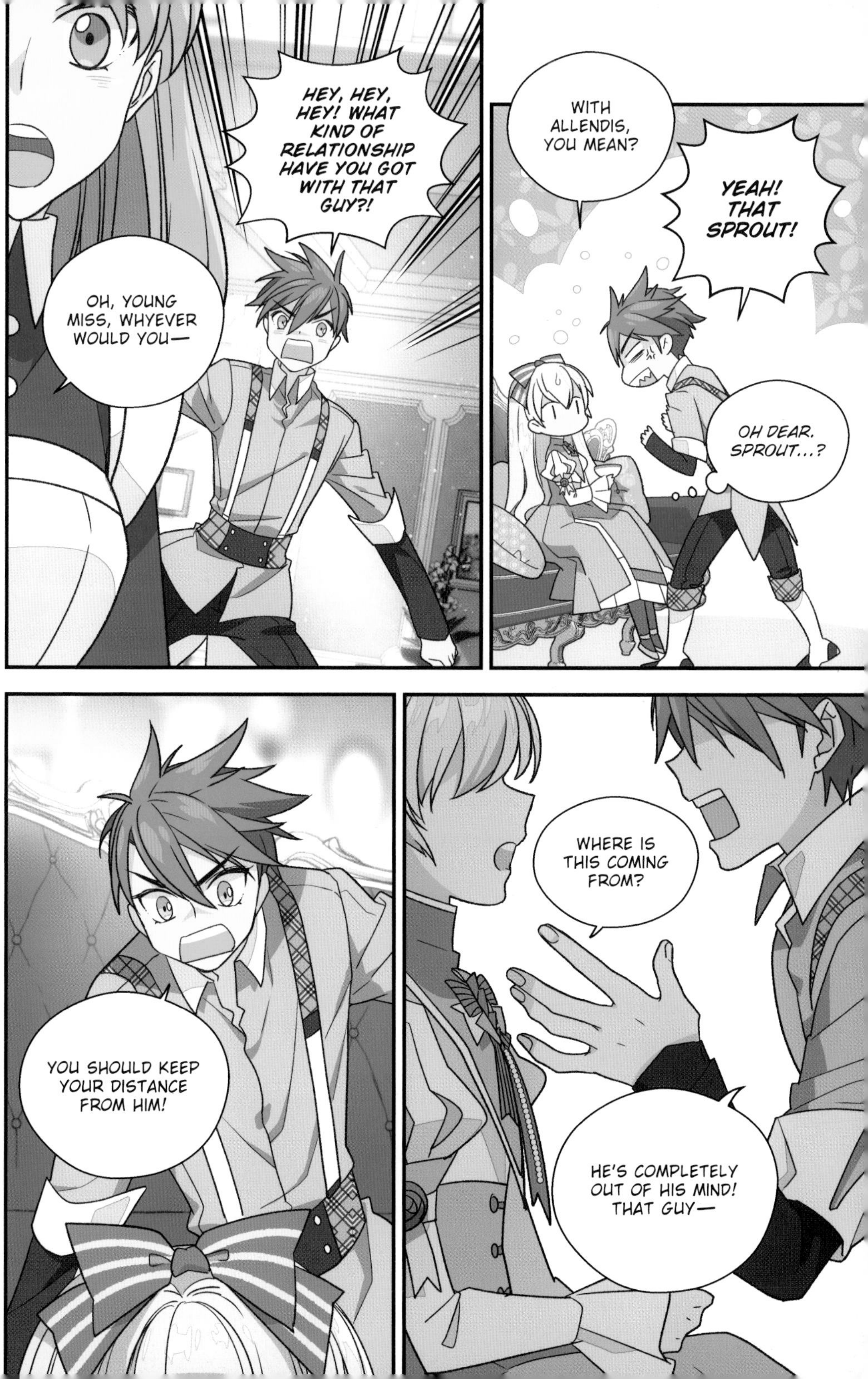
HEY, HEY, HEY! WHAT KIND OF RELATIONSHIP HAVE YOU GOT WITH THAT GUY?!
OH, YOUNG MISS, WHYEVER WOULD YOU—
WITH ALLENDIS, YOU MEAN?
YEAH! THAT SPROUT!
OH DEAR. SPROUT...?
YOU SHOULD KEEP YOUR DISTANCE FROM HIM!
WHERE IS THIS COMING FROM?
HE'S COMPLETELY OUT OF HIS MIND! THAT GUY—

BY "OUT OF HIS MIND," ARE YOU REFERRING TO ME, PERHAPS...

...YOUNG LORD RASS?

HAVE A SEAT, ALLEN. WOULD YOU LIKE TEA? IT'S LEMON BALM.

......

OF COURSE! THAT'S MY FAVORITE!

WAS EVERYTHING ALL RIGHT? I HEARD THERE MIGHT'VE BEEN SOME TENSION.

OH? NO, NOT AT ALL. I WAS SURPRISED, EVEN, AT HOW WELL WE UNDERSTOOD EACH OTHER.

THE YOUNG GENTLEMAN IS EXTREMELY PERCEPTIVE.

ISN'T THAT SO, LORD RASS?

NOT IF IT GETS ME LUMPED IN WITH THE LIKES OF YOU.

HOW SAD. AND I'D THOUGHT WE WERE THICK AS THIEVES ALREADY.

GAH! STOP IT!

MAYBE SOMETHING DID HAPPEN?

ALLEN LOOKS PERFECTLY UNPERTURBED, THOUGH...

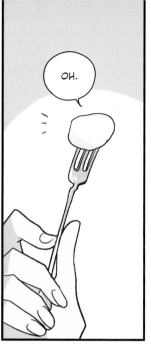

OH.

THAT REMINDS ME, ALLEN. DIDN'T YOUR LETTER MENTION A SPECIAL PRESENT?

HMM?

COME NOW— YOU STILL DIDN'T GET IT? I MUST SAY, THAT SADDENS ME SOMEWHAT.

HM? BUT I HAVEN'T RECEIVED ANYTHING, NOT EVEN WHITE CHOCOLATE...

THE GIFT IS BUT I, OF COURSE!

A MAN WHO IS WARM AND SWEET— JUST AS I SAID BACK THEN, NO?

WHAT? OH GEEZ, ALLEN.

BLAAARF

I MUST ASK, SPROUT—HAVE YOU LOST YOUR MARBLES?

YOU SEEM TO BE SPOUTING UTTER NONSENSE.

INDEED!

HAAH...

SURELY, THOUGH, TO BE ABLE TO MEET A FRIEND AFTER A LONG ABSENCE IS IN EVERY SENSE A SPECIAL GIFT.

IT'S WONDERFUL THAT YOU'VE RETURNED, ALLEN.

YES. LINA MUST'VE BEEN MISTAKEN.

THERE'S NO REASON FOR THESE TWO TO FIGHT OVER ME, RIGHT?

MORE PEOPLE KEEP COMING INTO MY LIFE, SO I CAN SPEND MY DAYS MUCH MORE ENJOYABLE THAN BEFORE—

YOUNG MISS.

A LETTER HAS ARRIVED FOR YOU.

OKAY, I'LL TAKE IT RIGHT HERE.

COULD IT BE FROM PAPA...?

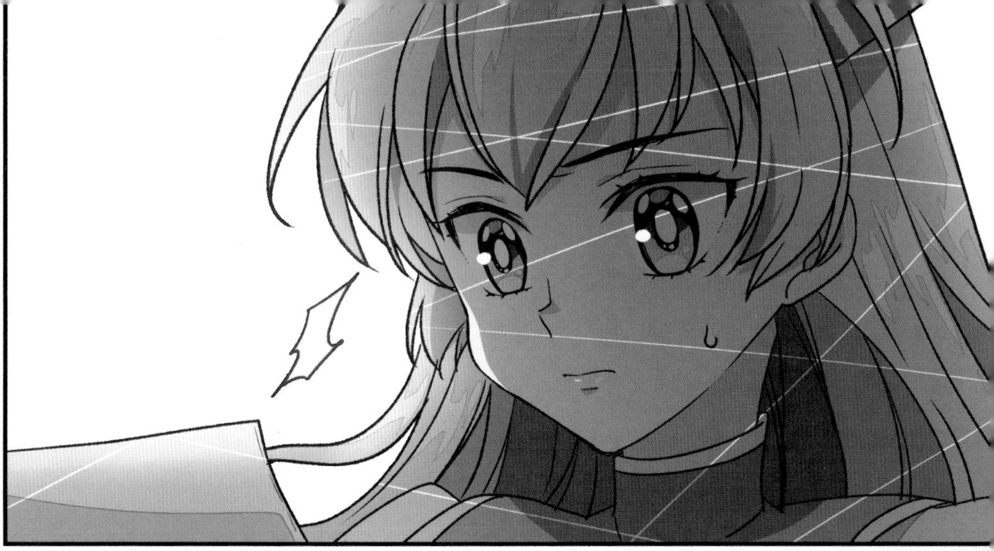

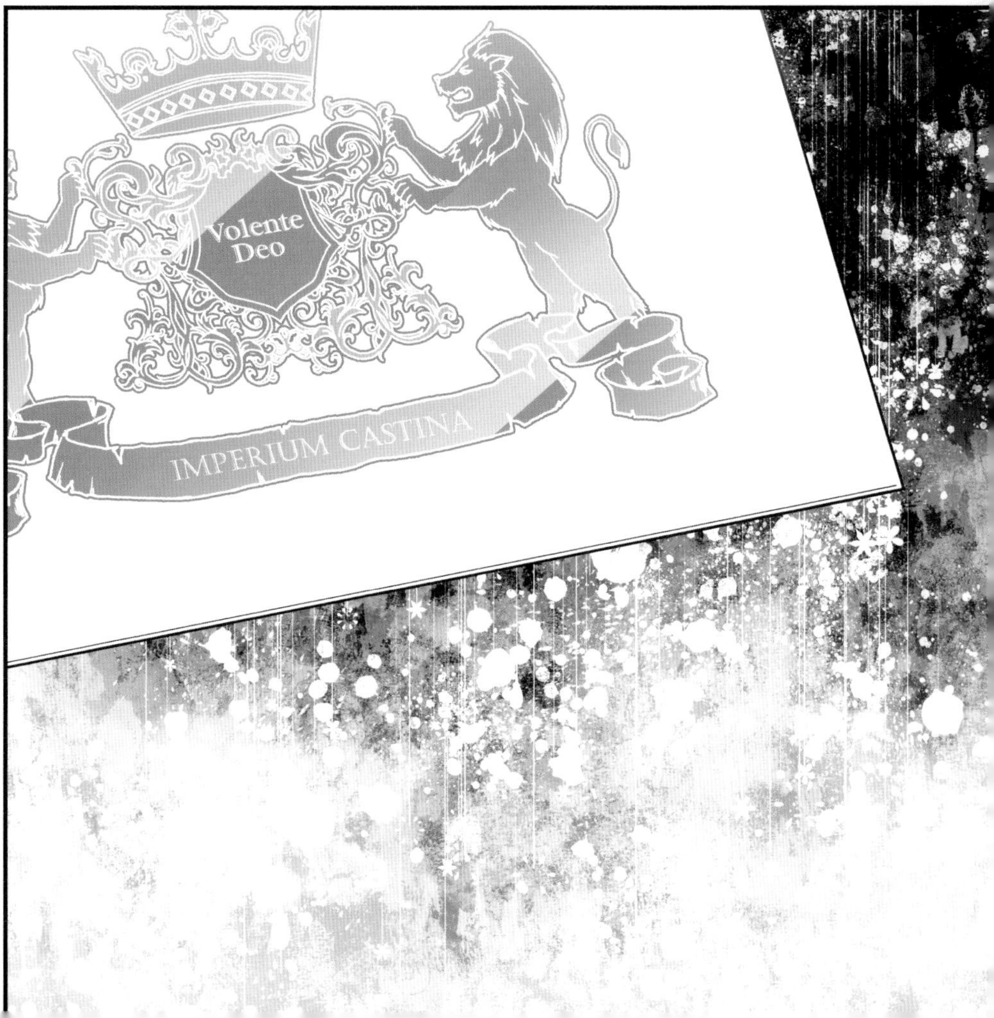

Volente Deo
IMPERIUM CASTINA

A CREST OF GOLDEN ROARING LIONS...!

Volente Deo

IMPERIUM CASTINA

IT'S FROM THE IMPERIAL FAMILY...!

......

WHAT'S WITH THAT EXPRESSION? DID YOU GET SOME BAD NEWS?

NO...... NOT EXACTLY.

WHY THE LONG FACE, THEN?

...A LETTER FROM THE IMPERIAL HOUSEHOLD SENT OUT AT THIS MOMENT CAN ONLY BE ABOUT ONE THING.

TWITCH

HUH? WHAT THING?

HONESTLY—FOR A YOUNG MASTER OF ONE OF THE NATION'S FOREMOST NOBLE HOUSES...

WHAT HAS THAT GOT TO DO WITH IT?!

THE RECOGNITION OF THE SOLE HEIR TO THE EMPIRE AS A FULLY GROWN ADULT WILL BE ANYTHING BUT AN UNDERSTATED AFFAIR.

IT'S SOON TO BE THE CROWN PRINCE'S COMING-OF-AGE CELEBRATION.

ALL THE CLERGY IN THE TEMPLES—TO SAY NOTHING OF THE ENTIRE CONTINENT—WILL HAVE EYES ON THE PROCEEDINGS.

THAT MISSIVE, UNDOUBTEDLY, IS AN ORDER FOR HER TO ATTEND...

...IN HER CAPACITY AS HIS HIGHNESS THE CROWN PRINCE'S FIANCÉE.

AH!

IT'S FINALLY COME. THE DEADLINE HIS MAJESTY SET FOR ME.

WHAT SHOULD I DO?

PAPA ISN'T EVEN BACK YET...

WILL I BE ABLE TO DO THIS ALONE?

DECLARING THAT I'LL INHERIT AND CARRY FORTH MY OWN FAMILY'S LINEAGE...

TIA.

ARE YOU ALL RIGHT?

YES... OF COURSE.

SUCH WARM HANDS.

ALLEN, YOU REALLY ARE THINKING OF ME ALWAYS...

THANK YOU.

I FEEL MUCH BETTER NOW.

GYAH!

HEY! WHAT DO YOU THINK YOU'RE DOING?

FROM THAT DAY ON...

SERIOUSLY, YOU TWO! WHADDAYA THINK YOU'RE DOING, LATCHING ON LIKE THAT?! LET GO!!

...THE CAPITAL, CASTILLA, THRIVED WITH THE ARRIVAL OF PEOPLE FROM ACROSS THE CONTINENT...

...ALL COME TO WITNESS THE ADVENT OF THE EMPIRE'S MORNING STAR INTO ADULTHOOD.

THE NATION'S COFFERS WERE FAR LESS THAN WELL LINED, OWING TO THE HARVEST SHORTFALLS...

...BUT THE IMPERIAL HOUSE NONETHELESS MADE SUMPTUOUS PREPARATIONS AND THREW OPEN THE LARDERS.

EVEN THOSE WHO HAD LEFT TO QUELL THE RIOTS AND ADMINISTER RELIEF WORK...

...GRADUALLY MADE THEIR WAY BACK TO THE CAPITAL CITY...

...EXCEPT FOR THE MARQUIS MONIQUE, OF WHOM THERE WAS NO NEWS TO BE HAD.

OH, YOUNG MISS!

THE SEAMSTRESS HAS ARRIVED FROM THE IMPERIAL PALACE TO TAKE MEASUREMENTS.

......

IT SEEMS WE MUST LEAVE IT AT THAT FOR TODAY.

GUESS SO, YEAH...

I'LL SEE YOU LATER, TIA.

I'M SORRY, YOU TWO.

SHEESH... SHE LOOKS MORE LIKE SHE'S GETTING LED TO AN EXECUTION THAN A CELEBRATION.

IS IT REALLY SUCH A TERRIFYING THING FOR HER?

SHE'D REALLY SEEMED TO BE CHEERING UP OVER THIS PAST YEAR TOO.

LOOKS LIKE SHE'S BACK TO SQUARE ONE...

SHE'S BOUND TO COLLAPSE AGAIN, AT THIS RATE.

...WHAT?

WHAT?

WHAT DID YOU SAY JUST NOW? TIA COLLAPSED?

SURE DID.

WHY?

WHAT DO YOU MEAN WHY? 'COS OF HER PLANS TO BE HER FAMILY'S—

GUESS I SHOULDN'T SAY MUCH...

......

WHEN WAS IT TIA COLLAPSED?

WHAT'S IT GOT TO DO WITH HER FAMILY NAME?

I'M NOT GONNA TELL YOU.

...HMM.

IS THAT SO?

SO YOU JUST WANTED TO ACT LIKE YOU HAD SOME INSIGHT, THEN.

IT MAKES SENSE, SEEING AS HOW LITTLE YOU KNOW TIA, I SUPPOSE.

WHATCHA SAY, SPROUT?!

AND?! WHAT ABOUT YOU?! ARE YOU TRYIN' TO PRY THINGS OUTTA ME 'COS YOU KNOW HER OH SO WELL!?

KEEP YOUR VOICE DOWN.

YOU KNOW I'M NOT THE ONE YOU OUGHT TO BE FIGHTING WITH, DON'T YOU?

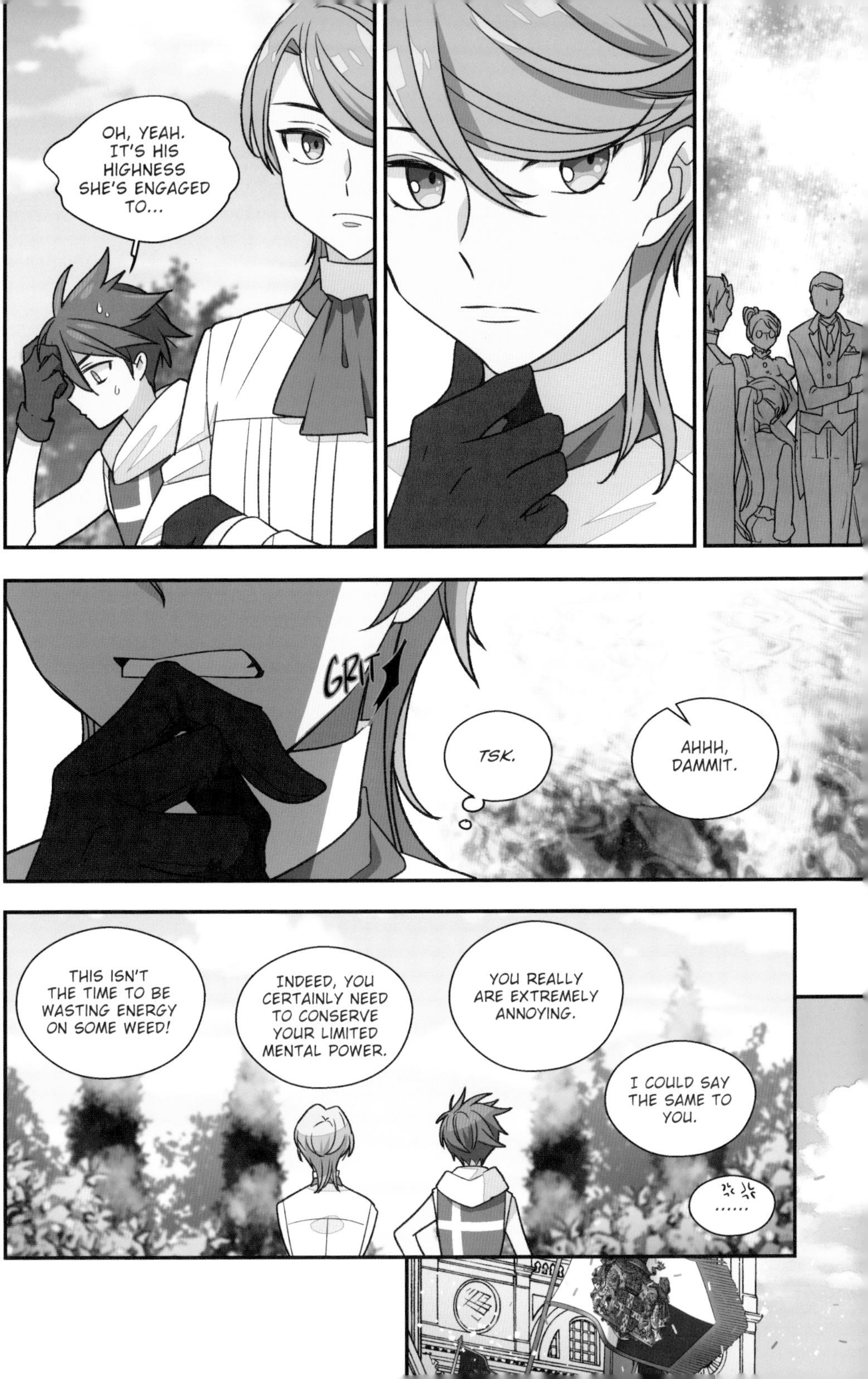
OH, YEAH. IT'S HIS HIGHNESS SHE'S ENGAGED TO...
GRIT
TSK.
AHHH, DAMMIT.
THIS ISN'T THE TIME TO BE WASTING ENERGY ON SOME WEED!
INDEED, YOU CERTAINLY NEED TO CONSERVE YOUR LIMITED MENTAL POWER.
YOU REALLY ARE EXTREMELY ANNOYING.
I COULD SAY THE SAME TO YOU.
......

THE COMING-OF-AGE CEREMONY IS ALREADY TOMORROW...

...AND YET...

NEARLY ALL THOSE WHO HAD BEEN DISPATCHED HAVE RETURNED...

...SO WHY, THEN, IS THERE NO NEWS OF PAPA?

IT'S NOT WAR— HE'S ONLY SURVEYING THE VARIOUS REGIONS OF THE EMPIRE...

...BUT I CAN'T STOP WORRYING...

YOUNG MISS.

THE YOUNG LORD VERITA IS HERE.

PAPA... PLEASE HURRY HOME.

I'M NOT SURE I CAN DO THIS ON MY OWN.

I'M SORRY FOR THE LATE HOUR. WERE YOU RESTING?

NO, IT'S FINE. ARE YOU DONE WITH ALL YOUR PREPARATIONS FOR TOMORROW, ALLEN?

WELL, I'VE LITTLE TO DO BESIDES ATTEND.

WHY DO YOU LOOK SO DOWN, MY LADY?

IT TEARS AT MY HEART.

IN FACT, I HEARD BY WAY OF LORD RASS...

...THAT YOU WERE UNWELL WHILE I WAS AWAY.

AND I RECALLED HOW URGENT YOU HAD BEEN—AS THOUGH YOU WERE BEING CHASED DOWN.

...I....

...SEE...

I'D SENT THAT LETTER, WORRIED THAT SUCH A THING MIGHT HAPPEN...

...BUT IT SEEMS IT WAS NOT HELP ENOUGH.

ALLEN...

...I CAUSED YOU WORRY EVEN WHEN YOU WERE SO FAR AWAY.

...I KNOW IT IS NOT THE IDEAL MOMENT AND YOUR PATIENCE MUST BE IN SHORT SUPPLY...

...BUT I THINK THIS NEEDS TO BE SAID.

...TIA.

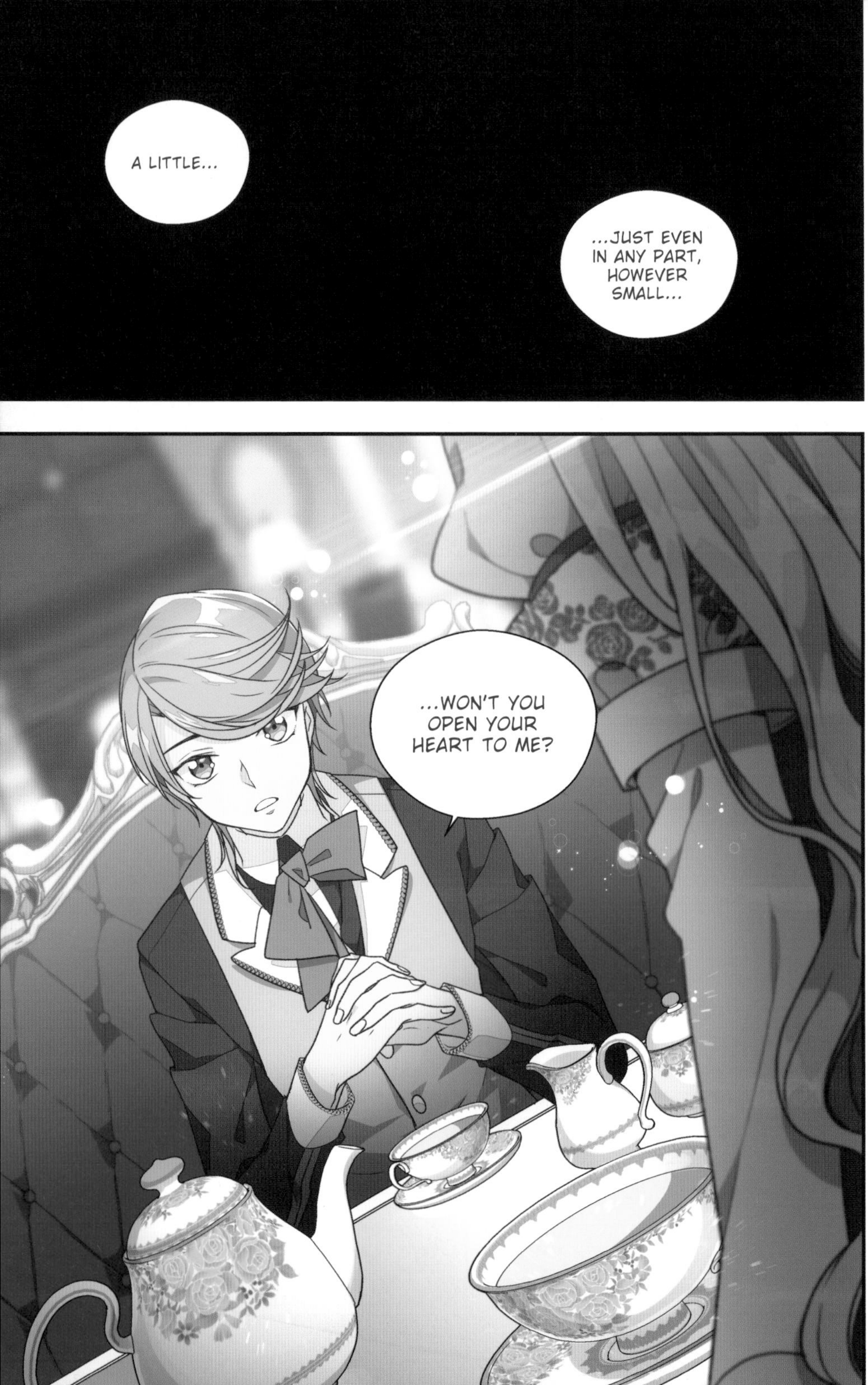
A LITTLE...
...JUST EVEN IN ANY PART, HOWEVER SMALL...
...WON'T YOU OPEN YOUR HEART TO ME?

AND THEREFORE, WHATEVER IT IS THAT PAINS YOU SO...

YOU'VE NEVER NOT BEEN KIND, BUT YOU'VE NEITHER REVEALED WHAT STIRS IN YOUR HEART'S DEPTHS.

...WHY YOU'RE SO AVERSE TO THE CROWN PRINCE, WHETHER YOU'RE TRYING TO CAST YOURSELF FREE OF THE IMPERIAL HOUSE...I KNOW NONE OF IT.

ALLEN...!

I'VE WATCHED OVER YOU ALL THIS WHILE, AND YET I KNOW SO LITTLE.

SOMETHING'S HURTING YOU...

...AND HOWEVER MUCH I WANT TO HELP, I AM POWERLESS BECAUSE I DON'T KNOW WHAT'S CAUSING IT.

WON'T YOU PLEASE TELL ME?

TELL ME WHAT IT IS YOU FEAR.

TELL ME HOW I CAN HELP.

ALLEN... TO THINK YOU FRET OVER ME SO MUCH.

WHAT SHOULD I DO?

WOULD IT BE OKAY...TO TELL ALLEN?

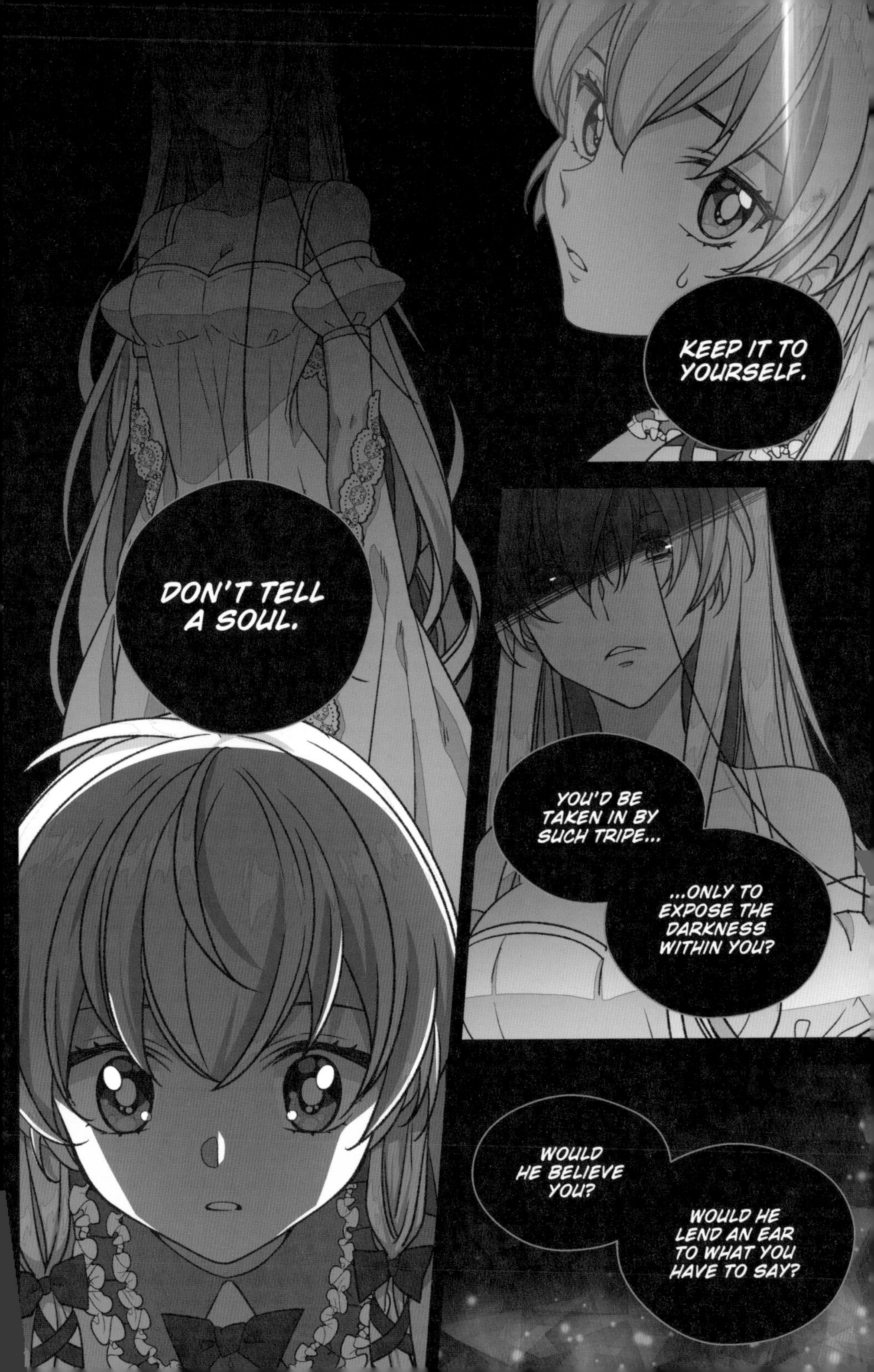
KEEP IT TO YOURSELF.
DON'T TELL A SOUL.
YOU'D BE TAKEN IN BY SUCH TRIPE...
...ONLY TO EXPOSE THE DARKNESS WITHIN YOU?
WOULD HE BELIEVE YOU?
WOULD HE LEND AN EAR TO WHAT YOU HAVE TO SAY?

WHAT IF YOU'RE ABANDONED YET AGAIN?

WHAT THEN?

PLEASE BELIEVE ME, TIA!

I'LL SHARE YOUR BURDEN!

ALLEN...WHOSE KINDNESS KNOWS NO LIMIT.

SHARE...MY BURDEN...?

IF YOU WOULD HEAR ME OUT...

YOU, WHO SAW WHAT I WAS HIDING AND ASKED HOW YOU COULD HELP INSTEAD OF PRETENDING NOT TO NOTICE...

YES...UNLESS I MUSTER MY COURAGE AND LAY IT ALL BARE, I WON'T BE ABLE TO MOVE ON FROM THIS PLACE.

I'D MADE UP MY MIND TO LIVE ON, TOGETHER WITH THE PEOPLE AROUND ME.

ALL RIGHT...
I'LL TELL YOU,
ALLEN.

EVEN IF IT IS
ALLEN...

BUT...

...HOW TO
GO ABOUT
IT?

...WOULD HE
EASILY ACCEPT
THE STORY OF
MY PAST?

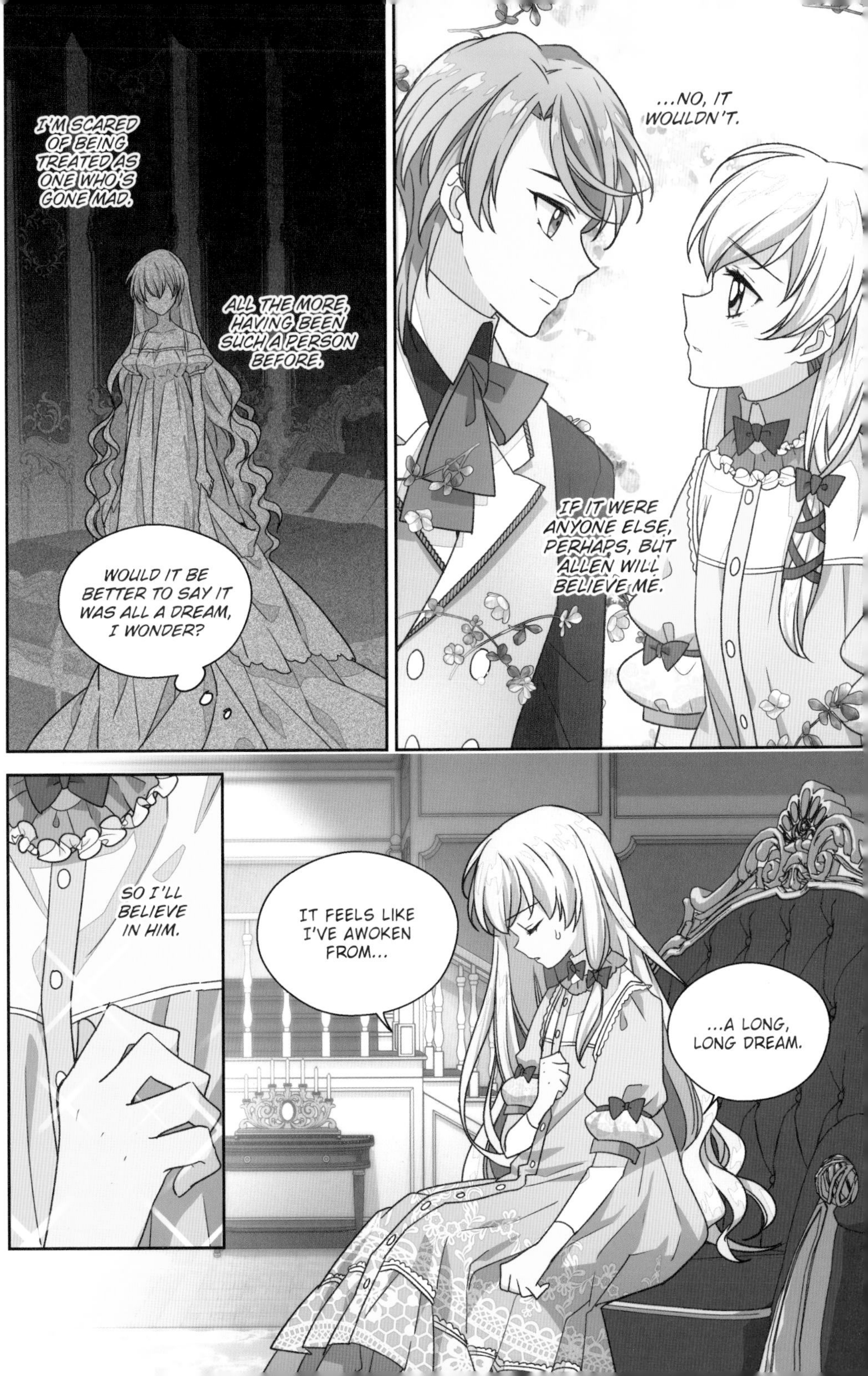
...NO, IT WOULDN'T.
I'M SCARED OF BEING TREATED AS ONE WHO'S GONE MAD.
ALL THE MORE, HAVING BEEN SUCH A PERSON BEFORE.
WOULD IT BE BETTER TO SAY IT WAS ALL A DREAM, I WONDER?
IF IT WERE ANYONE ELSE, PERHAPS, BUT ALLEN WILL BELIEVE ME.
IT FEELS LIKE I'VE AWOKEN FROM...
...A LONG, LONG DREAM.
SO I'LL BELIEVE IN HIM.

THIS CURRENT LIFE OF MINE...

...IS TIME I'VE BEEN BEQUEATHED A SECOND TIME AFTER DYING ONCE.

WHAT DO YOU MAKE OF THAT?

I EXPLAINED TO ALLEN THE PAST THINGS I'D EXPERIENCED BEFORE MY RETURN.

ABOUT THERE BEING A DIFFERENT CHILD OF PROPHECY...

...ABOUT SEEING JIEUN AND RUVE TOGETHER AND THE HURT I FELT...

...ABOUT THE MISCARRIAGE...

...ABOUT LEARNING OF MY FATHER'S DEATH AND RUNNING RUVE THROUGH WITH A HAIRPIN...

I LOVED HIS HIGHNESS DEEPLY...

...AND ENDURED GREAT HARDSHIP IN DOING SO.

I WAS ALONE...

...AND IN PAIN...

...AND IN HOPELESS DESPAIR.

I SOUGHT TO CAST MYSELF FREE SOMEHOW, BUT IN THE END...

I OPENED MY EYES TO FIND MYSELF RETURNED TO THE AGE OF TEN.

YEARS HAVE PASSED SINCE MY WAKING UP...

...YET I SEE NO WAY TO RECLAIM THIS DWINDLING TIME.

I WANT TO BE FREE OF THAT GRIM FUTURE...

...BUT NOW I DON'T KNOW. I DON'T KNOW WHAT I CAN DO TO ESCAPE.

I DON'T KNOW...

WILL HE... BELIEVE ME...? *clench*

...I SEE.

THAT MUST HAVE BURDENED YOU TERRIBLY, TIA.

SUCH SOOTHING WORDS...

I KNEW ALLEN WOULD...!

IT'S ALL RIGHT NOW, TIA.

DON'T LET YOUR AWFUL NIGHTMARE TROUBLE YOUR MIND.

YEAH...

IT'S ONLY JUST A DREAM, AFTER ALL.

...ALLEN?

BUT I MUST SAY, I'M A BIT SADDENED.

WHY ARE YOU TELLING ME ABOUT A DREAM ALL OF A SUDDEN?

THAT WASN'T WHAT I'D ASKED ABOUT.

DID YOU GO INTO ALL THAT BECAUSE YOU DON'T TRUST ME?

AH... I SEE.

ALLENDIS, YOU THINK I'M LYING.

FROM THE OUTSET, YOU...

YOU NEVER THOUGHT I WOULD OPEN MY HEART TO YOU IN THE FIRST PLACE.

ISN'T THAT SO?

NO, THAT'S NOT TRUE.

IT'S JUST, SINCE YOU'RE SO TROUBLED, I FIGURED IT MUST NOT BE EASY TO SAY WHAT'S REALLY ON YOUR MIND.

I WAS RIGHT...

I KNOW WHAT I SAID IS HARD TO BELIEVE.

I KNOW HOW ABSURD IT SOUNDS!

STILL, I THOUGHT THAT YOU OF ALL PEOPLE WOULD EARNESTLY LISTEN TO MY WORDS!

TIA!

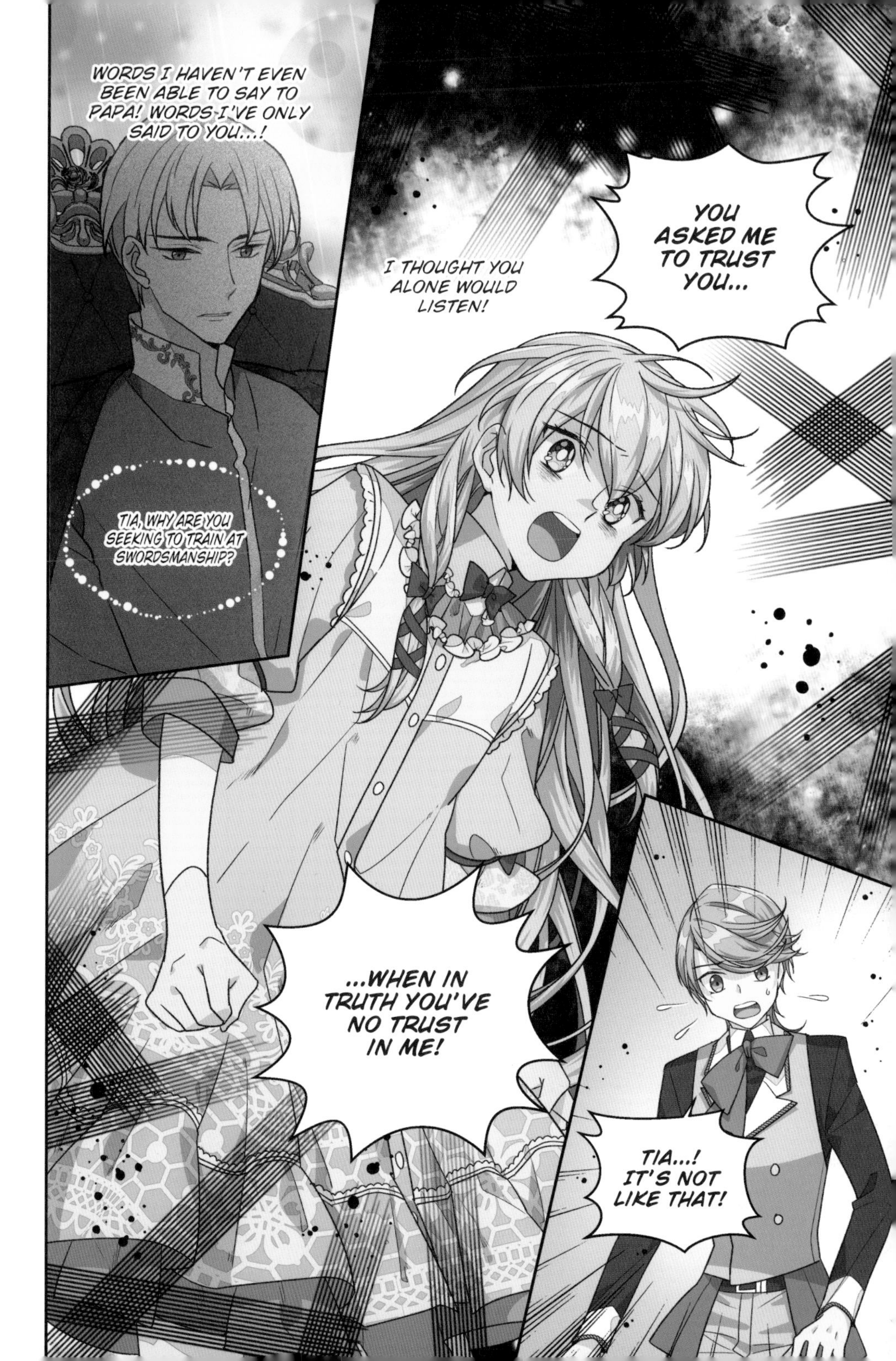
WORDS I HAVEN'T EVEN BEEN ABLE TO SAY TO PAPA! WORDS I'VE ONLY SAID TO YOU...!
TIA, WHY ARE YOU SEEKING TO TRAIN AT SWORDSMANSHIP?
YOU ASKED ME TO TRUST YOU...
I THOUGHT YOU ALONE WOULD LISTEN!
...WHEN IN TRUTH YOU'VE NO TRUST IN ME!
TIA...! IT'S NOT LIKE THAT!

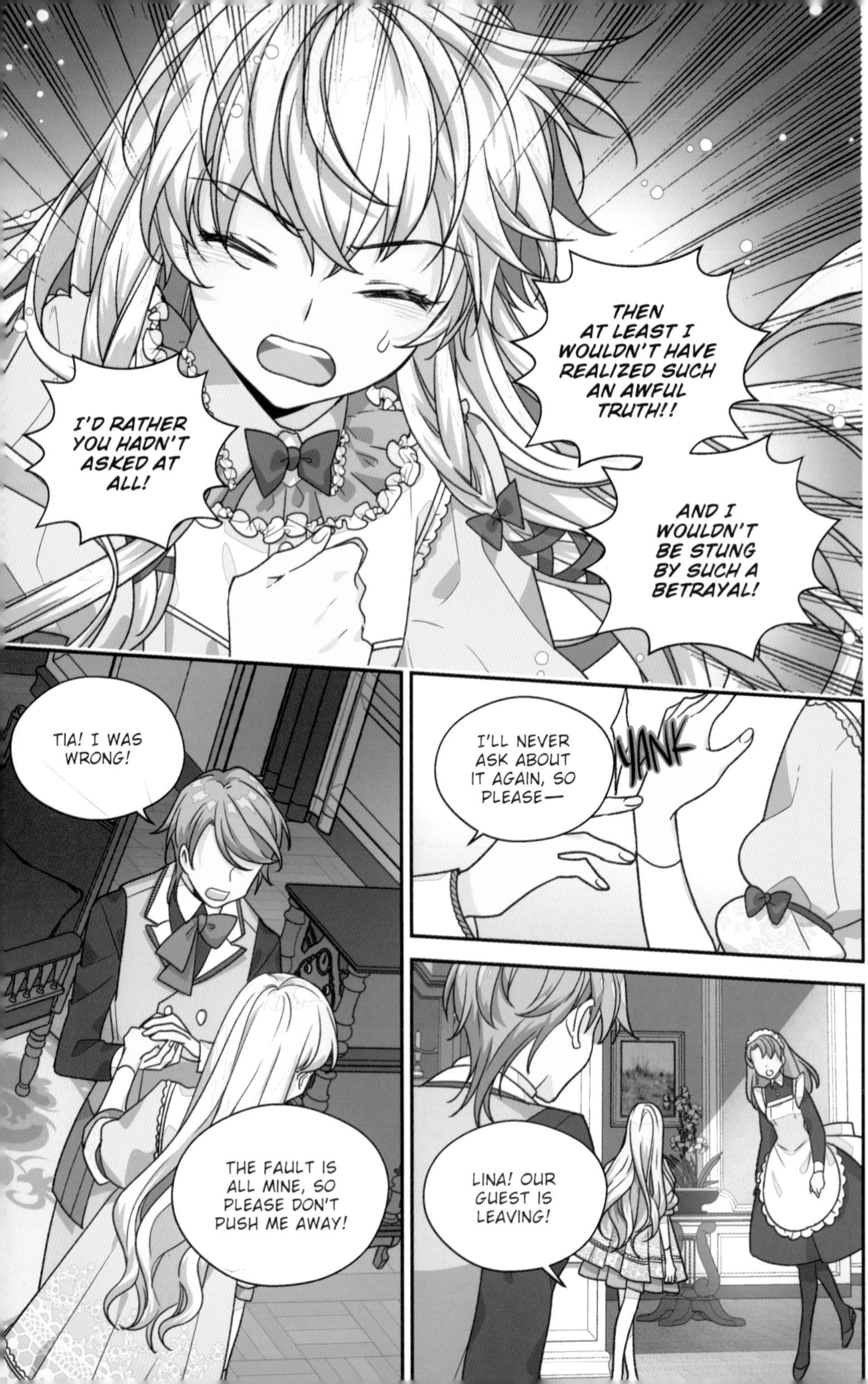

THEN AT LEAST I WOULDN'T HAVE REALIZED SUCH AN AWFUL TRUTH!!
I'D RATHER YOU HADN'T ASKED AT ALL!
AND I WOULDN'T BE STUNG BY SUCH A BETRAYAL!
TIA! I WAS WRONG!
I'LL NEVER ASK ABOUT IT AGAIN, SO PLEASE—
YANK
THE FAULT IS ALL MINE, SO PLEASE DON'T PUSH ME AWAY!
LINA! OUR GUEST IS LEAVING!

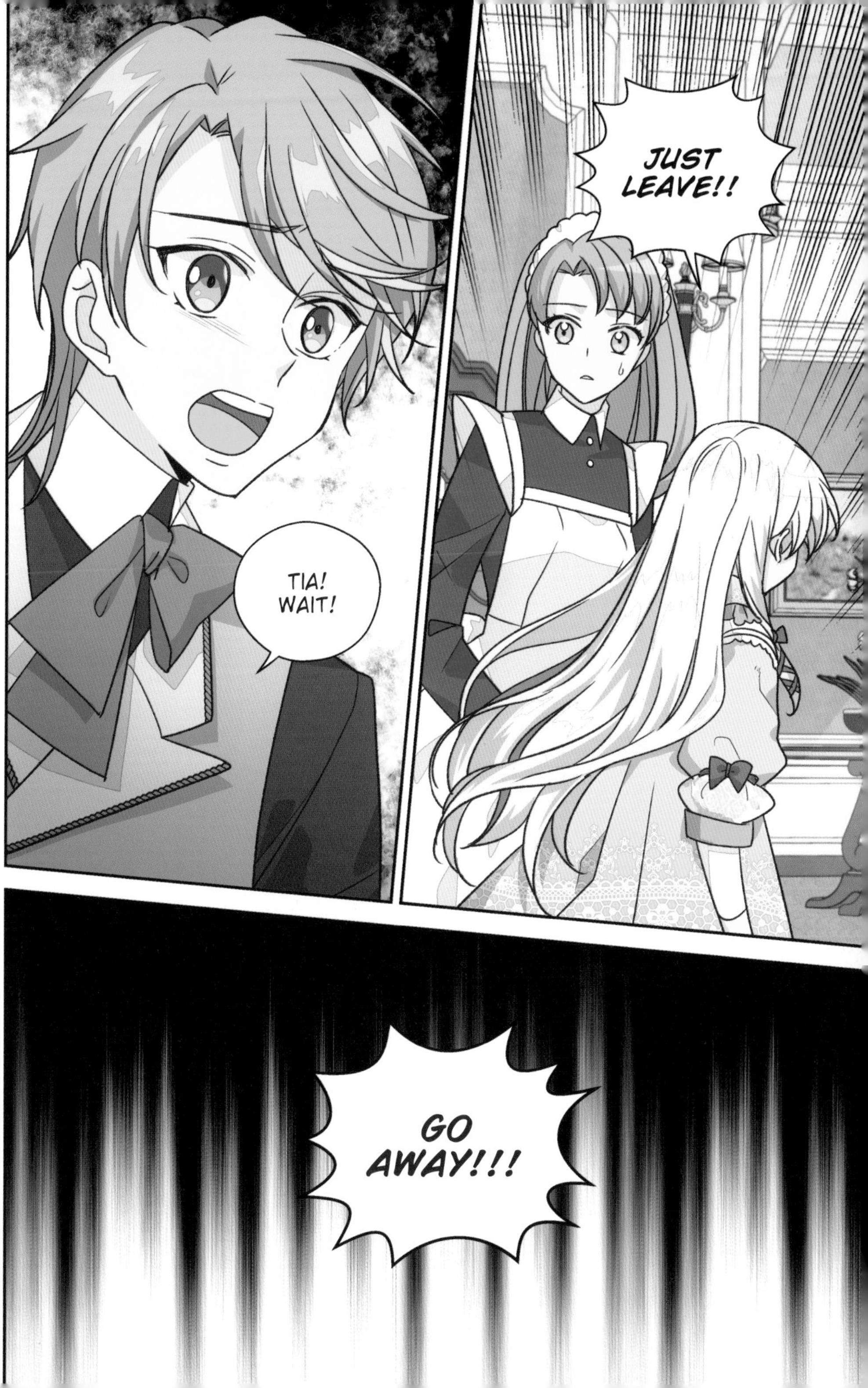
JUST LEAVE!!
TIA! WAIT!
GO AWAY!!!

The Abandoned Empress

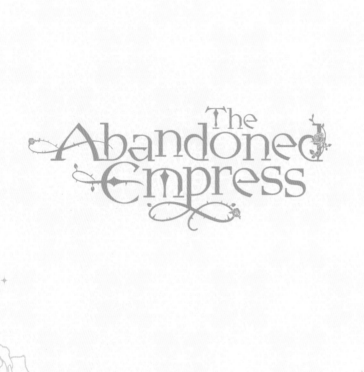

THE DAY OF THE CROWN PRINCE'S COMING-OF-AGE CELEBRATION

NO, SOMETHING BRIGHTER THAN THAT. YES, THAT'S THE ONE.

BRING THE RIBBONS.

WHERE'D THAT SAPPHIRE PIN GET TO?

COULD YOU RAISE YOUR FACE EVER SO SLIGHTLY, YOUNG MISS?

......

IT'S LIKE ALL THE VITALITY HAS LEFT THE YOUNG MISS.

WELL, YOU KNOW, YESTERDAY, YOUNG LORD VERITA...

GOODNESS, REALLY?

SHH!

TIA! I WAS WRONG!

AND STOP THAT GOSSIPING, YOU TWO!

PLEASE DON'T PUSH ME AWAY!

NOW... I DON'T CARE ANYMORE—

IT DOESN'T MATTER WHAT I DO...

...OR WHAT OCCURS TODAY...

LADY MONIQUE HAS ARRIVED.

Shf

MORNING STAR OF THE EMPIRE, HIS HIGHNESS THE CROWN PRINCE...

...I, ARISTIA LA MONIQUE, GREET THEE.

YOU, WHY...

WHY DOES SHE LOOK SO...?

...NEVER MIND. LET US GO.

PRESENTING CROWN PRINCE RUVELISS KHAMALUDIN SHANA CASTINA AND LADY ARISTIA LA MONIQUE!!

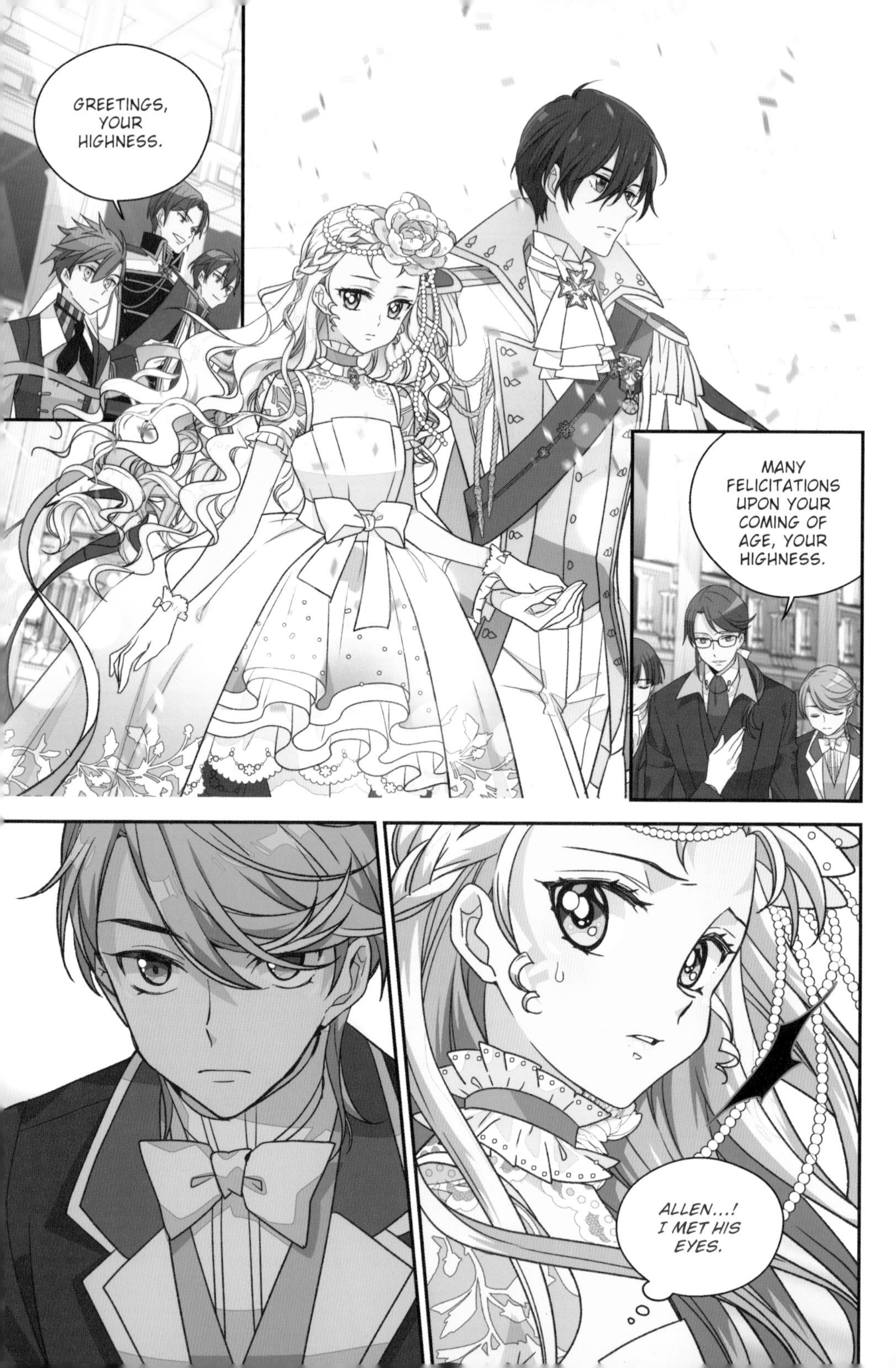
GREETINGS, YOUR HIGHNESS.
MANY FELICITATIONS UPON YOUR COMING OF AGE, YOUR HIGHNESS.
ALLEN...! I MET HIS EYES.

SO...THE YOUNG LORD VERITA.

HMM...

IN ACCORDANCE WITH THE CUSTOM OF THE IMPERIAL HOUSE...

...HEREBY IS THE CROWN PRINCE CORONATED UPON COMING OF AGE.

RECEIVE NOW, PRINCE, THIS CROWN AND BLADE.

CONGRATU-
LATIONS,
YOUR
HIGHNESS!!

FELICITATIONS
UPON HIS
HIGHNESS
THE CROWN
PRINCE!!

GLORY TO THE
EMPIRE OF
CASTINA!!

TO BE GREETED
BY SO MANY ON
MY COMING OF
AGE, I AM WELL
PLEASED.

I COULD
NOT POSSIBLY
EXPRESS MY
GRATITUDE TO
YOU ALL.

I HOPE THIS NIGHT'S BANQUET WILL BE ENJOYABLE TO ALL.

WE THANK YOU, YOUR HIGHNESS!!

WHEW...

IT'S SUFFOCATING.

THERE ARE SO MANY PEOPLE THAT I FEEL NAUSEOUS.

IF ONLY PAPA WERE HERE...

TIA.

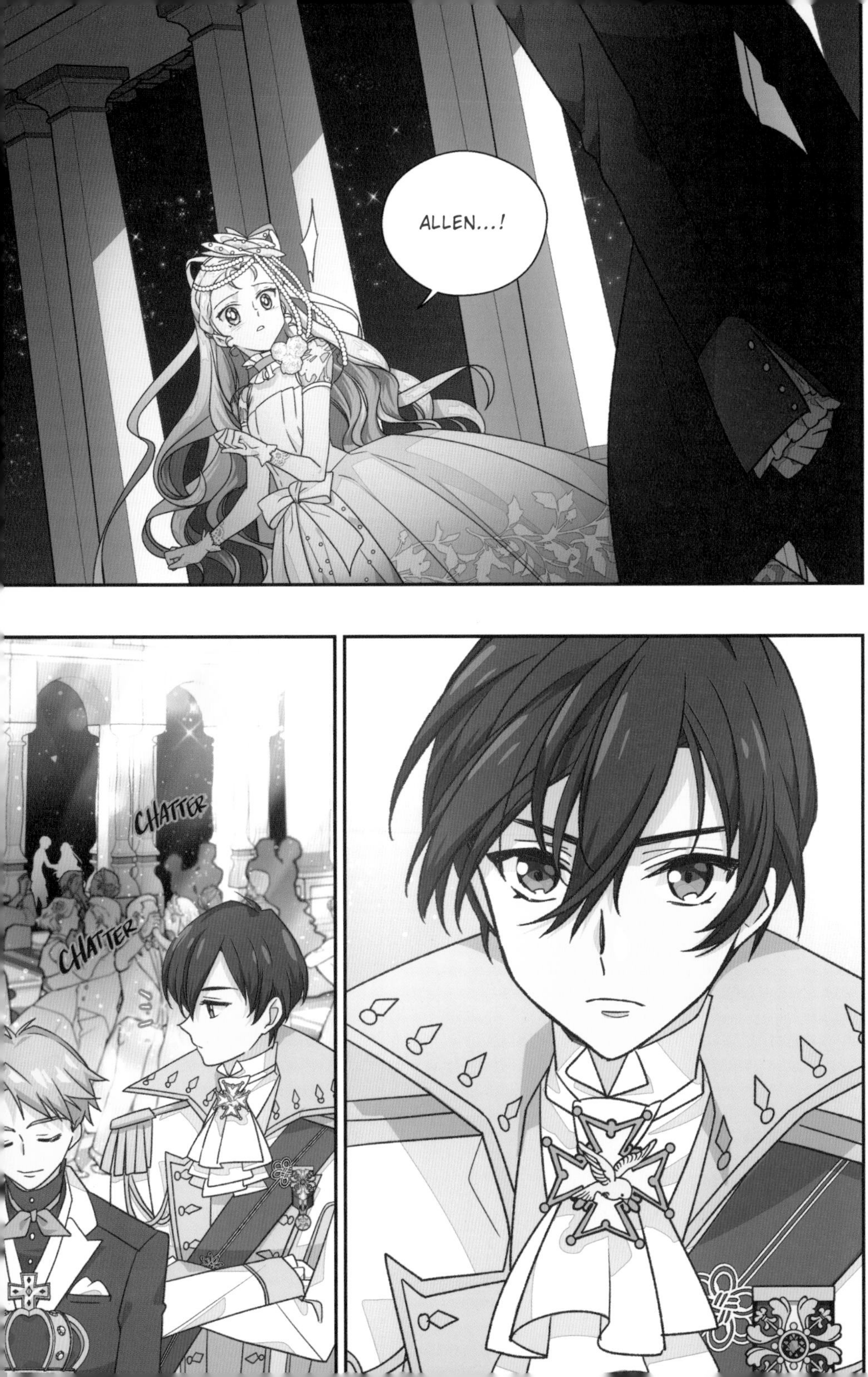
ALLEN...!
CHATTER
CHATTER

WHERE HAS THE YOUNG LADY MONIQUE GONE?

WE HAVE THE NEXT ITEM OF BUSINESS TO ATTEND TO.

TAP TAP

SHE EXCUSED HERSELF, SAYING SHE NEEDED TO NEATEN HER ATTIRE.

I COULD SEND SOMEONE—

NO NEED.

CHANCELLOR VERITA'S YOUNGER SON...

I ALSO HEARD THEY WERE FRIENDLY TOWARD EACH OTHER...

...THOUGH I'D PRESUMED IT WAS MERELY AMICABLE INTER-FACTION RELATIONS.

I HAD HEARD TALK PREVIOUSLY.

HE'D BEEN TRAINING IN SWORDSMANSHIP AT HOUSE MONIQUE.

BUT...

...DOES THAT...

...SEEM LIKE A "MERELY AMICABLE" RELATION-SHIP?

WHAT A RANGE OF EXPRESSIONS SHE SHOWS IN FRONT OF HIM.

TO ME, SHE SHOWS ONLY TWO—A VACANT EXPRESSION OR ONE FILLED WITH TERROR.

......

...WHAT IN THE WORLD ARE THEY UP TO OVER THERE?

HERE SHE COMES, YOUR HIGHNESS.

HAAH... WHAT AM I DOING?

MY EYES AREN'T NOTICEABLY RED, ARE THEY?

CLACK...

Y-YOUR HIGHNESS!

I APOLOGIZE DEEPLY FOR LEAVING MY STATION...

...THE REASON BEHIND THAT FACE...

THE SAME REACTION YET AGAIN...

...REQUEST THAT YOU BE MY FIRST DANCE PARTNER AFTER REACHING PROPER ADULTHOOD?

......

MAY I...

TODAY, I'LL HAVE YOU REVEAL...

...IT WOULD BE AN HONOR...

...YOUR HIGHNESS.

MUR

MUR

SHFT

OOH...

LADY MONIQUE HASN'T YET HAD HER SOCIETAL DEBUT, YES?

IT'S MY FIRST TIME SEEING HER—HOW SERENE AND MATURE SHE SEEMS!

WITH SUCH GRACE AND ELEGANCE, SHE TRULY IS A MATCH FIT FOR HIS HIGHNESS.

SHE'LL SURELY GROW INTO A MOST BEAUTIFUL LADY.

...COLD HANDS.

AND TIME PASSING IN WORDLESS SILENCE.

THE SAME REQUEST TO DANCE TO THE SAME TUNE AT THE SAME CEREMONY AS IN MY PAST.

IN THAT TIME, BEFORE I CROSSED BACK, IT WAS THIS VERY MOMENT...

TO ME, WANDERING ALONE IN A CROWD THAT REGARDED ME AS A SPECTACLE...

...WHEN I GAVE OVER MY WHOLE HEART TO HIM.

...HE WAS THE ONLY ONE WHO SMILED AND REACHED OUT HIS HAND TO ME.

EVEN IF IT WAS BUT PRESCRIBED FORMALITY, HE WAS THEN THE ONLY ONE THERE FOR ME.

WHAT DIFFERENCE IS THERE BETWEEN THE PAST AND NOW?

AM I SET UPON THE SAME PATH AS BEFORE, NO MATTER WHAT I DO?

THE ONE WHO STRIDENTLY RAILED AGAINST GOD AND FATE...

"PIONNIÈRE"...

...WILL THAT NAME PERHAPS COME TO NOTHING AFTER ALL?

A NAME RECEIVED FROM A GOD ONE HAS REJECTED...

HOW UNEXPECTED...

TO WHAT... IS YOUR HIGHNESS REFERRING?

THIS IS YOUR FIRST TIME DANCING, IS IT NOT?

I WOULDN'T HAVE IMAGINED YOU'D BE SO ADEPT AT IT.

IT IS BECAUSE I HAVE PRACTICED.

COUNTLESS TIMES IN THE PAST...

PRACTICED, YOU SAY?

YET I CAN SEE YOUR THOUGHTS ARE ELSEWHERE.

ARE YOU QUITE SURE IT'S NOT THAT THERE'S ANOTHER YOU'VE DANCED WITH TIME AND AGAIN TO RISE TO SUCH A LEVEL?

WHATEVER DOES YOUR HIGHNESS MEAN? I'D NOT DARE TO...

SO YOU SAY. THEN...

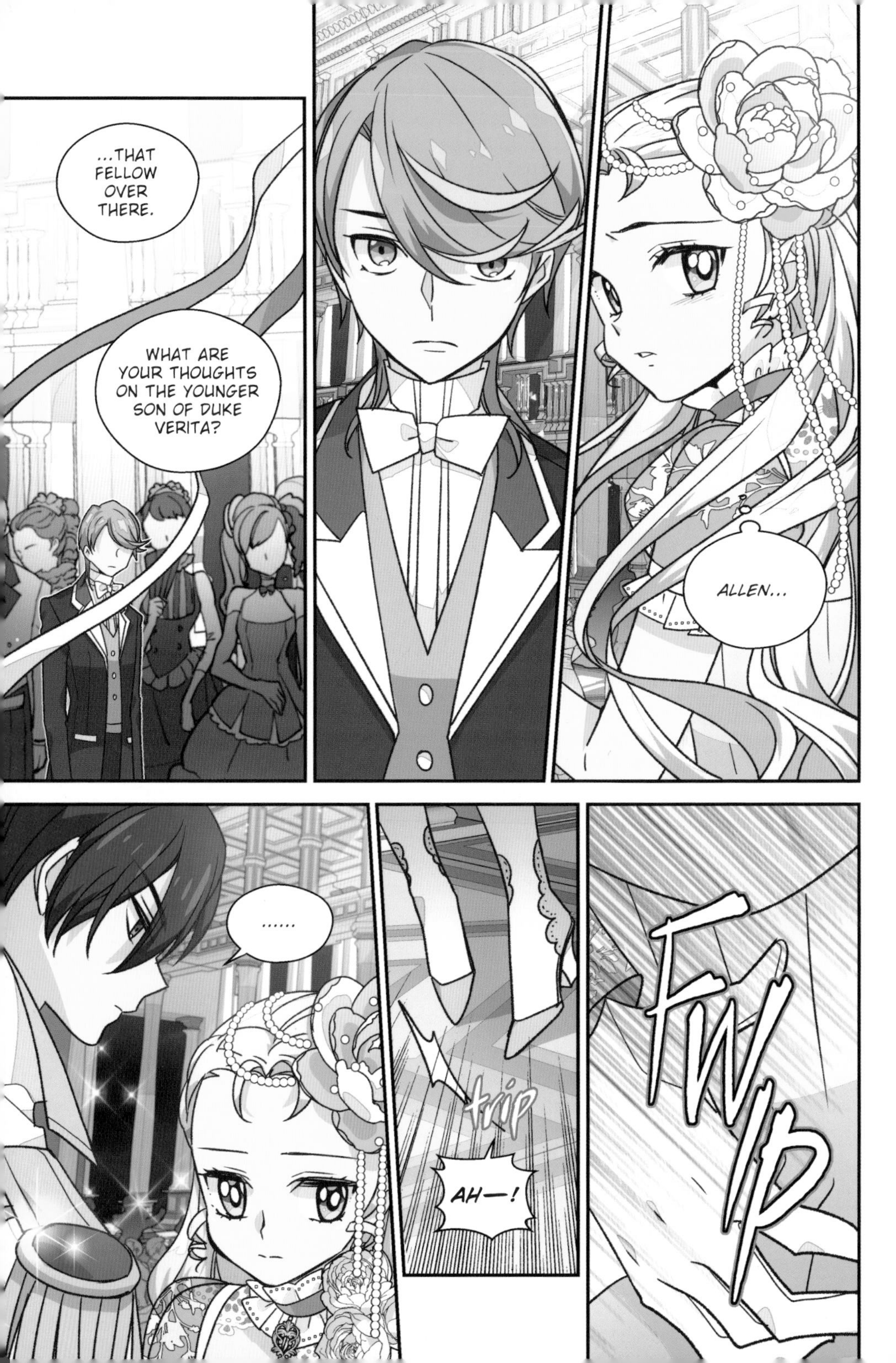
...THAT FELLOW OVER THERE.
WHAT ARE YOUR THOUGHTS ON THE YOUNGER SON OF DUKE VERITA?
ALLEN...
......
trip
AH—!
FWIP

CLASP

Y-YOUR HIGHNESS...

I'M QUITE DISPLEASED.

CLACK

CLAP CLAP CLAP CLAP CLAP CLAP CLAP CLAP CLAP CLAP CLAP

SUCH A HANDSOME PAIR!

LIKE THE TWO WERE MADE FOR EACH OTHER!

CLAP CLAP CLAP CLAP CLAP CLAP CLAP CLAP CLAP CLAP CLAP

MY THANKS TO YOU FOR JOINING MY FIRST PROPER DANCE UPON COMING OF AGE.

THE HONOR IS WHOLLY MINE... YOUR HIGHNESS.

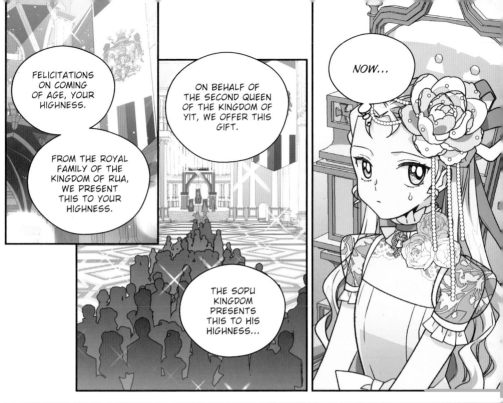

FELICITATIONS ON COMING OF AGE, YOUR HIGHNESS.

FROM THE ROYAL FAMILY OF THE KINGDOM OF RUA, WE PRESENT THIS TO YOUR HIGHNESS.

ON BEHALF OF THE SECOND QUEEN OF THE KINGDOM OF YIT, WE OFFER THIS GIFT.

THE SOPU KINGDOM PRESENTS THIS TO HIS HIGHNESS...

NOW...

...WHEN SHALL I TRY TO INFORM HIS MAJESTY?

ONCE THE PROCESSION OF FELICITATIONS IS FINISHED, PEOPLE WILL BEGIN MOVING ELSEWHERE, SO IF I COULD FIND A QUIET SPOT—

YOU.

Y-YES? YOU SPOKE, YOUR HIGHNESS?

I'VE BEEN WONDERING...

WHY IS IT THAT YOU ARE AFRAID OF ME?

A-AFRAID, YOUR HIGHNESS? I'M NOT SURE—

YOU KNOW FULL WELL WHAT I'M TALKING ABOUT.

PERHAPS...

...SOME RECOLLECTION OF YOUR YOUTH HAS RETURNED TO YOU?

......?

MY YOUTH...?

IT SEEMS THAT'S NOT IT.

OR...

...COULD IT BE OWING TO YOUR NAME, *PIONNIERE*?

HOW DID—?!

HOWEVER FLEETING AN EVENTUALITY, YOU'VE EMERGED A BEARER OF DIVINE RIGHT TO THE THRONE.

AND IT WAS A NAME GIVEN BY AN ORACLE AS WELL.

...WHAT DOES YOUR HIGHNESS HAVE A MIND TO DO WITH ME?

......

THOUGH HIS MAJESTY ORDERED IT BE KEPT UNDER WRAPS, IT'S NEVER LONG BEFORE I FIND OUT ABOUT ALL THE AFFAIRS OF THE IMPERIAL HOUSEHOLD.

PRINCESS OF THE COURT.

...IT WOULD BE SAFEST TO PUT YOU IN THE POSITION DIRECTLY BENEATH THAT OF CROWN PRINCESS.

!!

A PRINCESS OF THE COURT...!

THAT WOULD MEAN I'D THEN BECOME AN IMPERIAL CONSORT...!

I'M BUT A THORN IN HIS SIDE, AFTER ALL...

...SO OF COURSE HE'D HAVE CONSIDERED IT!

BUT SEEING HOW YOUR HOUSE HAS LOYALLY SERVED THE EMPIRE...

...I WOULD ALLOW YOU TO MAINTAIN THEIR NOBLE STATUS.

WOULD THAT DO?

...WHAT IS THAT EXPRESSION? AREN'T YOU SATISFIED?

THE GOOD NAME OF YOUR HOUSE CAN THUSLY CONTINUE.

WAS IT NOT SULLYING YOUR REPUTATION YOU WERE WORRIED ABOUT?

NO...

I'VE MADE A GRAVE ERROR...! I SHOULDN'T HAVE ASKED HIM THAT!

EVEN IF I'M ALLOWED TO MAINTAIN MY RANK AS A NOBLE, THE FACT THAT JIEUN WILL SHOW UP WON'T CHANGE!

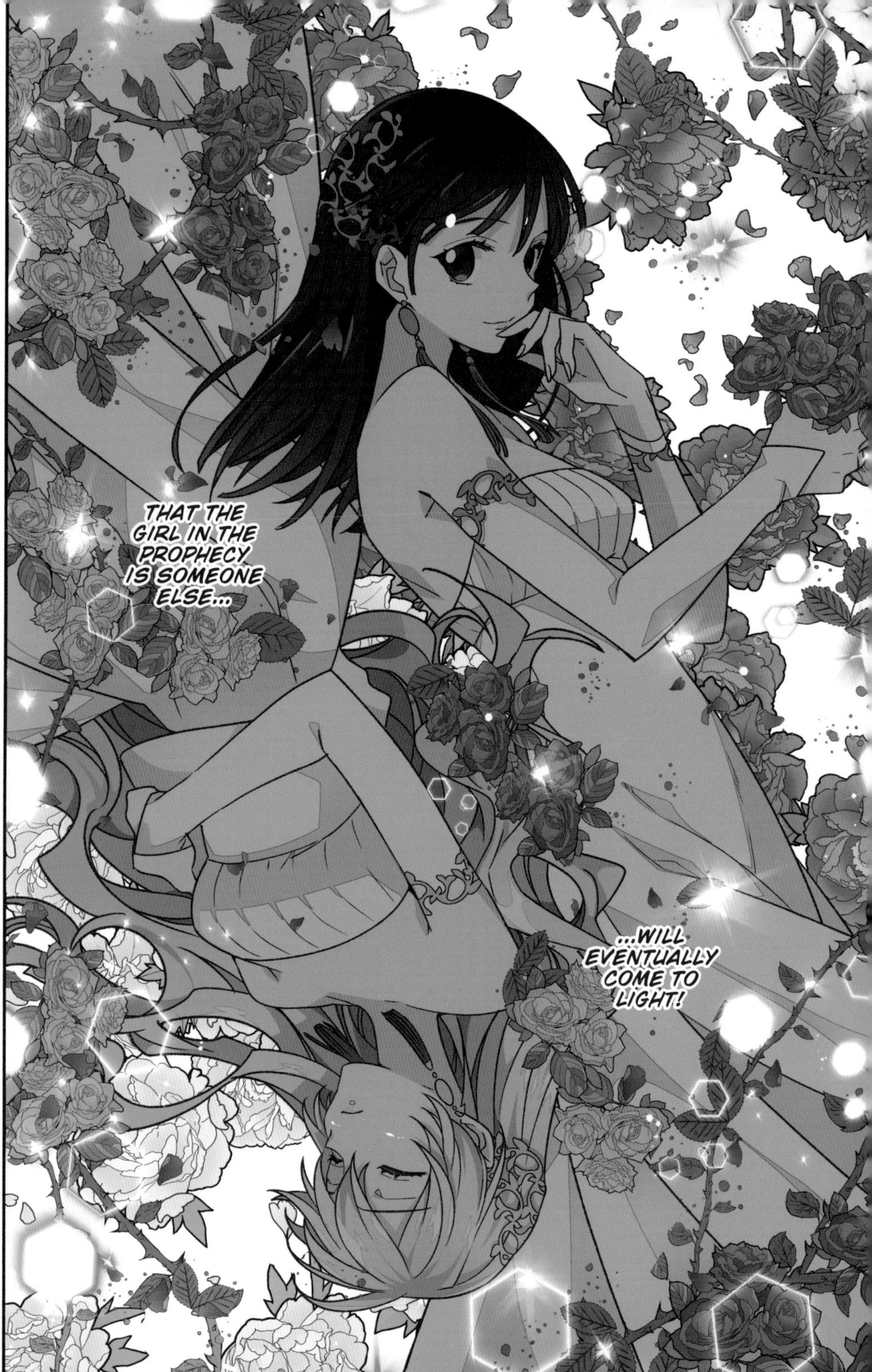
THAT THE GIRL IN THE PROPHECY IS SOMEONE ELSE...
...WILL EVENTUALLY COME TO LIGHT!

IF THINGS HAD GONE AS PLANNED, I WAS SUPPOSED TO ANNOUNCE MY INTENT TO INHERIT MY FAMILY'S LINEAGE TODAY.

BUT DOING SO NOW WILL BE DIRECTLY REJECTING THE CROWN PRINCE'S CONSIDERATION!

IS THIS HOW IT ALL ENDS...?!

......

Y-YOUR HIGHNESS...

I—

MUR MUR

HM?

CLAMOR

CLAMOR

IT SEEMS SOMEONE HAS ARRIVED.

......?

FL

AP

CLACK

189

MY MOST SINCERE APOLOGIES FOR MY LATE ARRIVAL.

SUN OF THE EMPIRE, HIS MAJESTY THE EMPEROR, AND MORNING STAR OF THE EMPIRE, HIS HIGHNESS THE CROWN PRINCE, I GREET THEE.

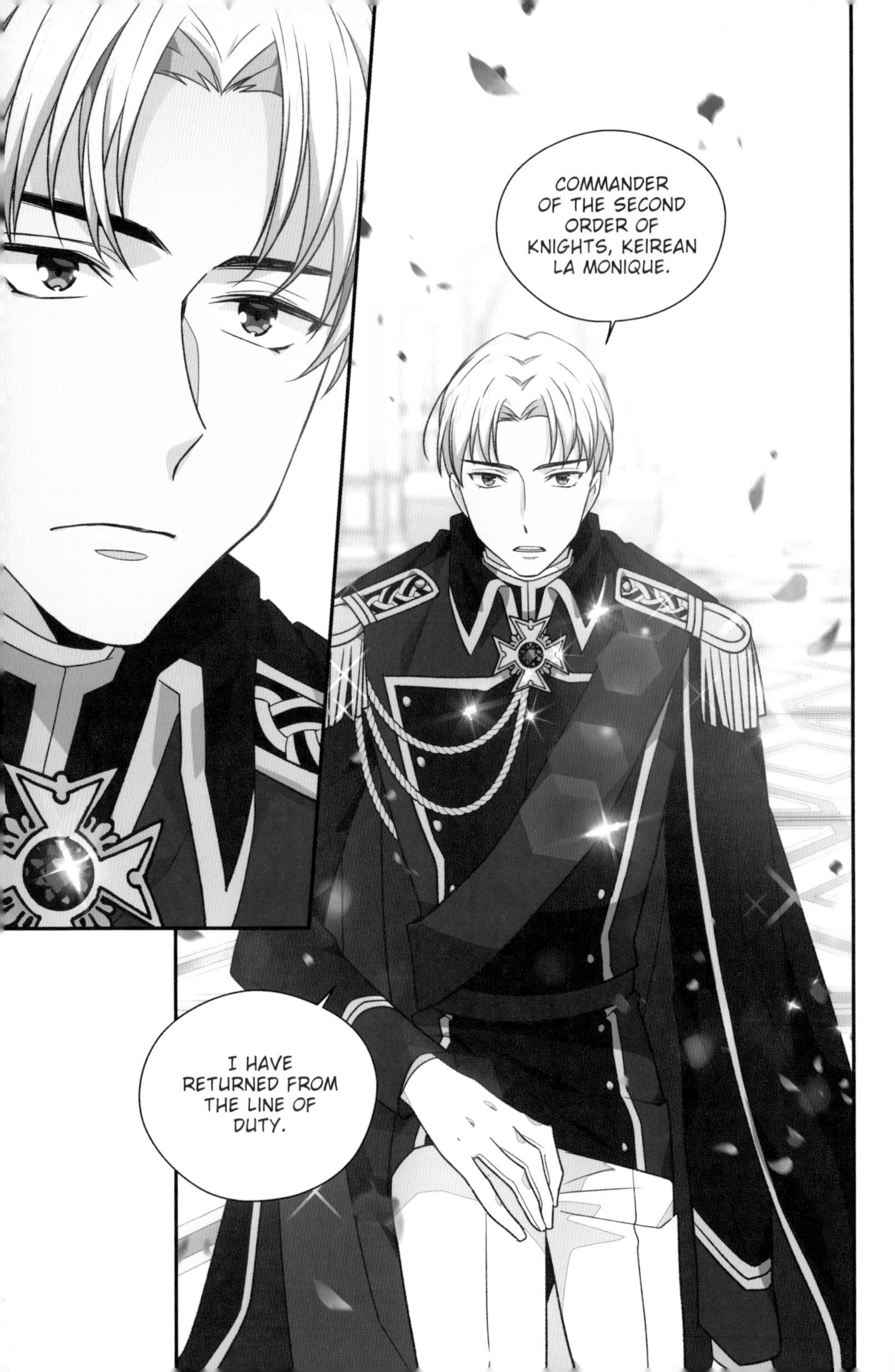
COMMANDER OF THE SECOND ORDER OF KNIGHTS, KEIREAN LA MONIQUE.
I HAVE RETURNED FROM THE LINE OF DUTY.

PAPA...!

HE'S SAFELY RETURNED...!!

MARQUIS, YOU'VE COME AT LAST.

WE WERE VERY CONCERNED WHEN WE HEARD THAT ALL NEWS OF YOUR WHEREABOUTS HAD GONE SILENT.

MY SINCERE APOLOGIES, YOUR MAJESTY.

FOCUSED IN MY HURRY TO ARRIVE IN TIME FOR HIS HIGHNESS'S COMING-OF-AGE CELEBRATION, I WAS UNABLE TO SEND WORD IN ADVANCE.

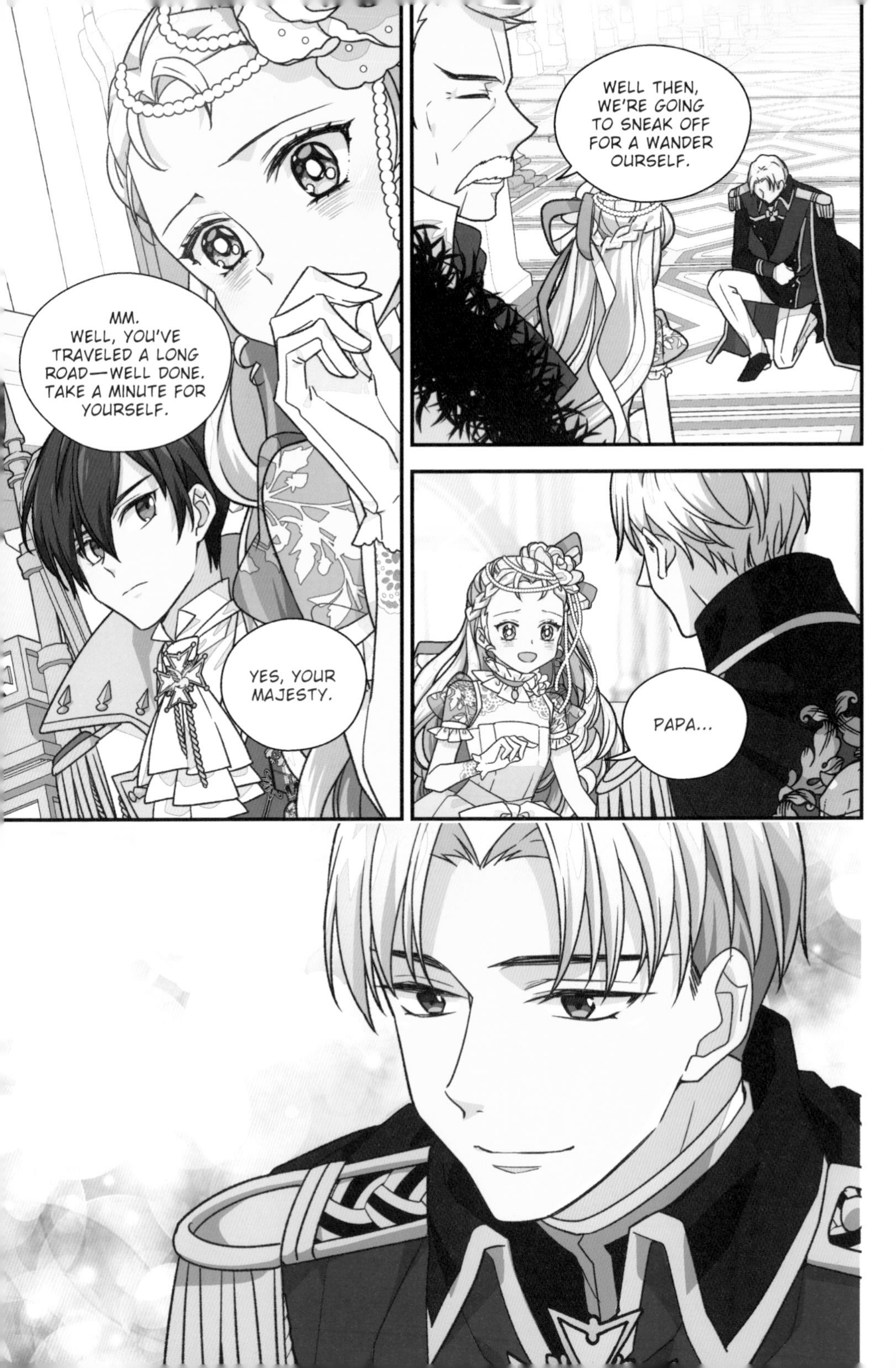
WELL THEN, WE'RE GOING TO SNEAK OFF FOR A WANDER OURSELF.
MM. WELL, YOU'VE TRAVELED A LONG ROAD—WELL DONE. TAKE A MINUTE FOR YOURSELF.
YES, YOUR MAJESTY.
PAPA...

CHATTER

CHATTER

TIA... HAVE YOU BEEN WELL?

IT SEEMS YOU'VE GROWN SINCE I LAST SAW YOU.

YOU LOOK A BIT WEATHERED, PAPA.

IT'S WONDERFUL THAT YOU'RE SAFELY BACK...

YOU CAN'T KNOW HOW I LONGED TO SEE YOU.

TRULY... HOW MUCH I...

TEAR

THAT A YOUNG LADY ALL GROWN UP SHOULD LET HER TEARS FLOW SO.

THERE ARE OTHERS WHO MIGHT FIND FAULT IN IT.

WHY, MARQUIS. IT SEEMS YOUR DAUGHTER IS STILL YOUNG.

IT IS JUST AS HIS MAJESTY SAYS.

I SUPPOSE IT MAY BE THAT I'VE BEEN LAX IN LETTING HER ACT AS A CHILD.

YOU? PERMITTING CHILDISHNESS? WHY, IT'S DIFFICULT FOR US TO IMAGINE.

AS YOUR MAJESTY WELL SEES, MY LITTLE ONE IS BY NO MEANS PERFECT.

SHE MIGHT FALL SHORT OF THE REQUIREMENTS INVOLVED IN ATTENDING THE CROWN PRINCE, WHO HAS COME OF AGE.

!

OH-HOOO... SO THEN?

I'VE BEEN GIVING THOUGHT AS TO WHOM I SHOULD CHOOSE AS HEIR TO OUR FAMILY LINE, YOUR MAJESTY.

BULLY, YOU OLD DOG! ON THE HUNT TO MARRY AGAIN, ARE YOU?

WHO WILL BE THE LUCKY LADY?

OHH?

THAT'S NOT IT, YOUR MAJESTY.

THAT'S SOMETHING I WOULD NEVER DO, AND...

...SOMETHING THAT "COULD NEVER BE DONE"...

...AS YOUR MAJESTY WOULD BE WELL AWARE OF, CORRECT?

YOU'RE NOT SAYING...!

MY DAUGHTER IS MY ONE AND ONLY CHILD, NOW AND EVER AFTER.

YOU'VE DECIDED SHE'LL UNDERGO THAT?

ARE YOU CERTAIN? BUT YOU'D ALWAYS REFUSED TO DO SO...

WE SHALL SEE, YOUR MAJESTY.

HEIR...

...TO HOUSE MONIQUE.

WAS THIS THE REASON BEHIND HER SWORDSMANSHIP TRAINING?

IT'D SEEM SO.

THAT MUST BE THE REASON FOR HER REACTING THAT WAY ALL THIS TIME.

HE'S WILLING TO GO SO FAR...

MARQUIS.

THIS SEEMS RATHER SUDDEN.

I ACKNOWLEDGE MY ERSTWHILE INATTENTIVENESS TOWARD THE YOUNG LADY.

BUT NEITHER SHOULD YOU MISTAKE IT FOR MY REJECTING HER.

IRRESPECTIVE OF ALL ELSE, THE YOUNG LADY WAS CHOSEN AS MY COMPANION BY GOD.

AND NOW, SHE'S TO BE YOUR HEIR?

I'VE NO EXCUSE TO OFFER, HIGHNESS.

LET US THEN TAKE THE CONVERSATION BACK UP AT SOME LATER TIME.

SUCH A TALK IS NOT SUITED TO THE OCCASION, I SHOULD THINK.

YOUR MAJESTY, THERE ARE MANY ONLOOKERS HERE.

LET US DISCREETLY TAKE OUR LEAVE.

AH, YES, LET'S.

MARQUIS AND THE ESTEEMED YOUNG LADY, UNTIL NEXT TIME.

whisper
whisper

KEIREAN!

WELL HELLO, OLD FRIEND. A BIT LATE TO THE PARTY, AREN'T YOU?

DON'T YOU KNOW HOW MUCH ANXIETY YOU WERE GIVING THE YOUNG LADY, MAKING HER WAIT FOR YOU?

INDEED, IT WOULD SEEM I DID.

I MEAN, KAISIAN MADE HIS WAY BACK ON TIME—AND MEANWHILE THE COMMANDER OF THE WHOLE ORDER FALLS OFF THE FACE OF THE PLANET?

...HMM.

DO I ASK HER ABOUT WHAT I SAW EARLIER?

SEEMS LIKE SOMETHING'S UP BETWEEN HER AND THE SPROUT...

DID YOU LOSE WEIGHT? YOUR CHEEKBONES ARE LOOKING KIND OF...

NO, NO. IF ANYTHING, I'VE GAINED WEIGHT.

HEE HEE!

......

EH...

?

CHATTER

CHATTER

IN A SINGLE NIGHT'S TIME, SO MANY THINGS HAPPENED, AND SO MANY THOUGHTS FOLLOW IN THEIR WAKE.

FROM THIS DAY FORWARD...

...I WONDER WHAT LIES IN STORE FOR ME.

I WONDER WHERE I'M HEADED...

TIA, IT'S ME.

PAPA.

YOU SHOULD REST, PAPA. YOU MUST BE TIRED...

I'M FINE.

NOTHING IN PARTICULAR.

I'D SAY YOU'RE THE ONE WHO LOOKS TIRED.

DID SOMETHING HAPPEN?

I'M SORRY FOR BEING SO LATE IN MY RETURN AND SENDING NO WORD.

I'M SURE YOU WERE WORRIED.

BUT YOU'VE RETURNED SAFE AND SOUND.

HOW I'VE MISSED PAPA'S EMBRACE...

MY MIND IS AT EASE WHEN HE'S HOLDING ME LIKE THIS.

RIGHT NOW, IT'S EVERYTHING I NEED.

HERE, I'LL STAY BY YOUR SIDE UNTIL YOU'RE ASLEEP.

The Abandoned Empress

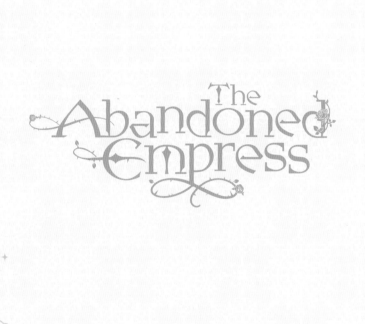

CHATTER
CHATTER

BUSTLE

NGH...

BUSTLE

...WHY'S IT
SO NOISY...?

MMM...

WAH!!

HEY!!

CHATTER CHATTER

KER

CHAK

!!

WHAT IN THE
WORLD IS GOING
ON OUT THERE
SO EARLY...?

JABBER

JABBER

JABBER

JABBER

AH! IT'S THE YOUNG MISS!

GOOD MORNING, YOUNG MISS!

YOUNG MISS, DID YOU SLEEP WELL?

IT'S SO GOOD TO SEE THE YOUNG MISS AGAIN!

WE'VE RETURNED RATHER LATE, HAVEN'T WE?!

IT'S A RELIEF TO SEE THE YOUNG MISS IN SUCH GOOD HEALTH!

EVERYONE...!

THE WHOLE ORDER HAS SAFELY RET—

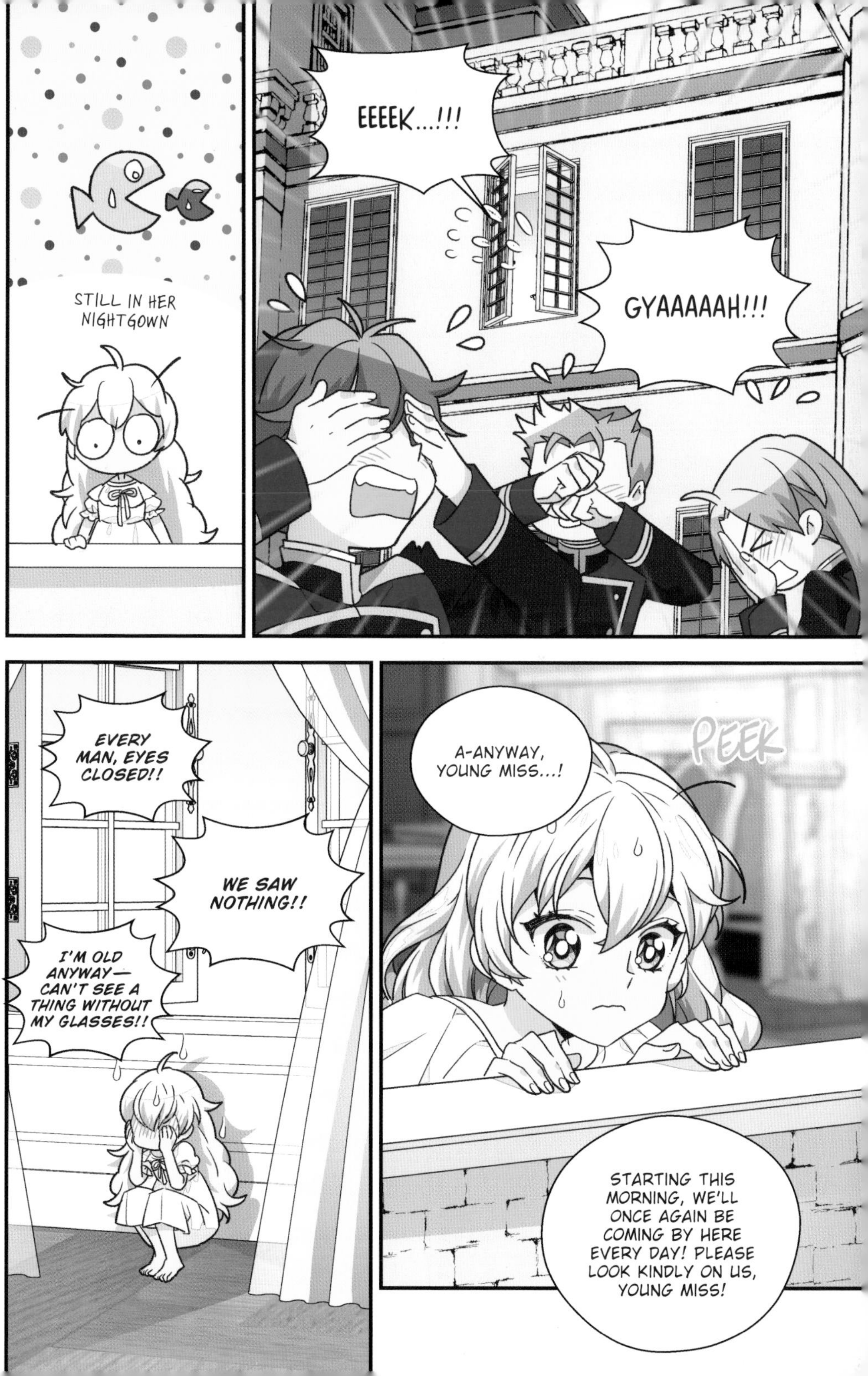
STILL IN HER NIGHTGOWN
EEEEK...!!!
GYAAAAAH!!!
EVERY MAN, EYES CLOSED!!
WE SAW NOTHING!!
I'M OLD ANYWAY—CAN'T SEE A THING WITHOUT MY GLASSES!!
PEEK
A-ANYWAY, YOUNG MISS...!
STARTING THIS MORNING, WE'LL ONCE AGAIN BE COMING BY HERE EVERY DAY! PLEASE LOOK KINDLY ON US, YOUNG MISS!

WE HOPE TO SEE THE YOUNG MISS ON THE TRAINING FIELD LATER!!

I HEAR PEOPLE'S VOICES EACH MORNING....

COME ALONG NOW.

...AND WHEN I GO DOWNSTAIRS, PAPA IS THERE WAITING.

HOWEVER NARROWLY, IT HAS BEEN RESTORED TO ME—MY PRECIOUS EVERYDAY LIFE.

TIA.

ABOUT YESTERDAY...

REGARDING THE MATTER WITH HIS MAJESTY AND HIS HIGHNESS...

YOU NEEDN'T WORRY TOO MUCH ABOUT IT.

BUT, PAPA...

YOU MIGHT FEEL UNEASY THAT WE WERE UNABLE TO SETTLE THE MATTER RIGHT THEN...

...BUT HIS MAJESTY UNDERSTANDS WELL ENOUGH THAT HE WON'T DO ANYTHING TOO RASH OR ABRUPT.

LIKEWISE HIS HIGHNESS, OF COURSE.

FOR NOW, GET SOME REST.

OVERSEEING THE HOUSEHOLD ALONE MUST HAVE BEEN A FATIGUING TRIAL, WASN'T IT?

YES...

I WOULD LOVE TO REST IF I COULD.

HOWEVER...

...WILL EVERYTHING SIMPLY FALL INTO PLACE WITH PAPA'S DECLARATION OF AN HEIR?

ONE MUST FIRST BECOME A KNIGHT TO BE NAMED AS HEIR TO HOUSE MONIQUE...

...AND ONLY THE HEIR IS ABLE TO INVOKE THAT—

THE SOLE MEANS BY WHICH I COULD ESCAPE THE ENGAGEMENT...

—THAT VOW...

HMM? WHAT'S THAT, YOUR HIGHNESS?

HE MEANS TO INVOKE IT.

IT'S NOTHING.

SHE RECALLS NOTHING ABOUT OUR ENCOUNTER IN OUR CHILDHOOD...

...YET SHE FEARS JUST THE SIGHT OF ME...

...AND WHILE SHE OFTEN PASSED THE TIME IN HIS MAJESTY'S GARDEN...

...SHE'D BEEN OF A MIND TO BECOME HEIR TO HOUSE MONIQUE?

AND GOING SO FAR AS TO USE THE VOW?

WHAT THOUGHTS ARE RUNNING THROUGH YOUR HEAD?

ALL THIS, JUST TO ESCAPE ANY ENTANGLEMENT WITH ME?

YET I STILL HAVEN'T HEARD THE REASON FROM YOU...

HUP!

KLA NG

HYA!

WELL...

CAN'T SIT BY AND LET MY BROTHER GET RUSTY IS ALL.

IS THAT RIGHT? YOU SEEM A BIT TOO RESTLESS FOR THAT TO BE THE LONG AND SHORT OF IT...

WHAT'S THE OCCASION? ASKING FOR A SPARRING MATCH WITH REAL BLADES AND ALL.

YOU WEREN'T GOING TO VISIT THE MONIQUE ESTATE TODAY?

URK...!

...I MEAN, EVEN IF I WENT...

...TODAY, I'D JUST BE IN THE WAY.

217

HMM.

I SUPPOSE. THE COMMANDER IS BACK IN ANY EVENT.

I SUPPOSE I CAN VOLUNTEER SOME TIME TO PLAY TOGETHER WITH MY KID BROTHER.

I'M NOT JUST YOUR "KID BROTHER." I'M A PRODIGY, OKAY—

BONK✦

OW!

DAAAAAZE

DAAAAAAAAAAAAAAZE

WHAT'S THE YOUNG MISS UP TO OVER THERE?

SHE'S BEEN SEEMING A BIT OUT OF SORTS OF LATE.

SHE DOESN'T APPEAR SICK OR INJURED, BUT...

DAaAZE

WHAT IN THE WORLD HAPPENED WHILE WE WERE AWAY...?

TIA.

YOU REMEMBER I'D SAID IT'D BE FINE TO REST TODAY, DON'T YOU? WON'T YOU GO BACK INSIDE?

PAPA.

NO, NO— I WANTED TO SEE EVERYBODY.

IT'S JUST... KIND OF...

WELL, PAPA AND ALL THE KNIGHTS OF THE ORDER HAVE RETURNED...

...SO MY DAYS TOO HAVE RETURNED TO HOW THEY ONCE WERE...

I HAVE ROOM TO BREATHE NOW, BUT INSTEAD I FEEL EXHAUSTED.

IT RATHER FEELS LIKE MY HEART...

TO THINK BEING AT HOME WOULD BECOME A HARDSHIP IN ITSELF.

HAAH...

...WANTS TO GET AWAY...

AH, NO!

I'M JUST TALKING NONSENSE! I ONLY MEANT...!

IT'S JUST THAT I'M A BIT FATIGUED...

......

THEN, TIA, SHALL WE GET AWAY?

WE HAVE OUR COUNTRYSIDE ESTATE SOME TWO DAYS FROM THE CAPITAL...

...SO IF YOU'D LIKE, YOU AND I CAN GO ON A TRIP.

HOUSE MONIQUE'S RURAL MANOR...!

TOGETHER WITH PAPA...!!

THIS EXISTENCE I'VE LIVED EVER IN REACH OF THE CAPITAL...

...AND THE EXISTENCE THAT I'VE NONETHELESS HARBORED A DEEP WISH FOR...

IF I COULD CAST MYSELF FREE OF IT...

...TOGETHER WITH PAPA...

YES, I'D LIKE THAT.

THERE'S NOTHING WE'VE FORGOTTEN?

ALAN, HAVE THE REST OF THE YOUNG MISS'S LUGGAGE SENT ON A SEPARATE WAGON BEHIND THE CARRIAGE.

DO TAKE CARE OF YOURSELF ON THE LONG ROAD AHEAD ON YOUR JOURNEY, YOUNG MISS.

OKAY. I'LL SEE YOU WHEN I GET BACK.

IN THESE THREE YEARS SINCE CROSSING BACK IN TIME, I'VE FOUGHT MY HARDEST...

...BUT WHEN IT COMES TO THE ROLLING WHEEL OF FATE TO WHICH I WAS TIED BY GOD...

...HOW FAR CAN I TRULY STRAY?

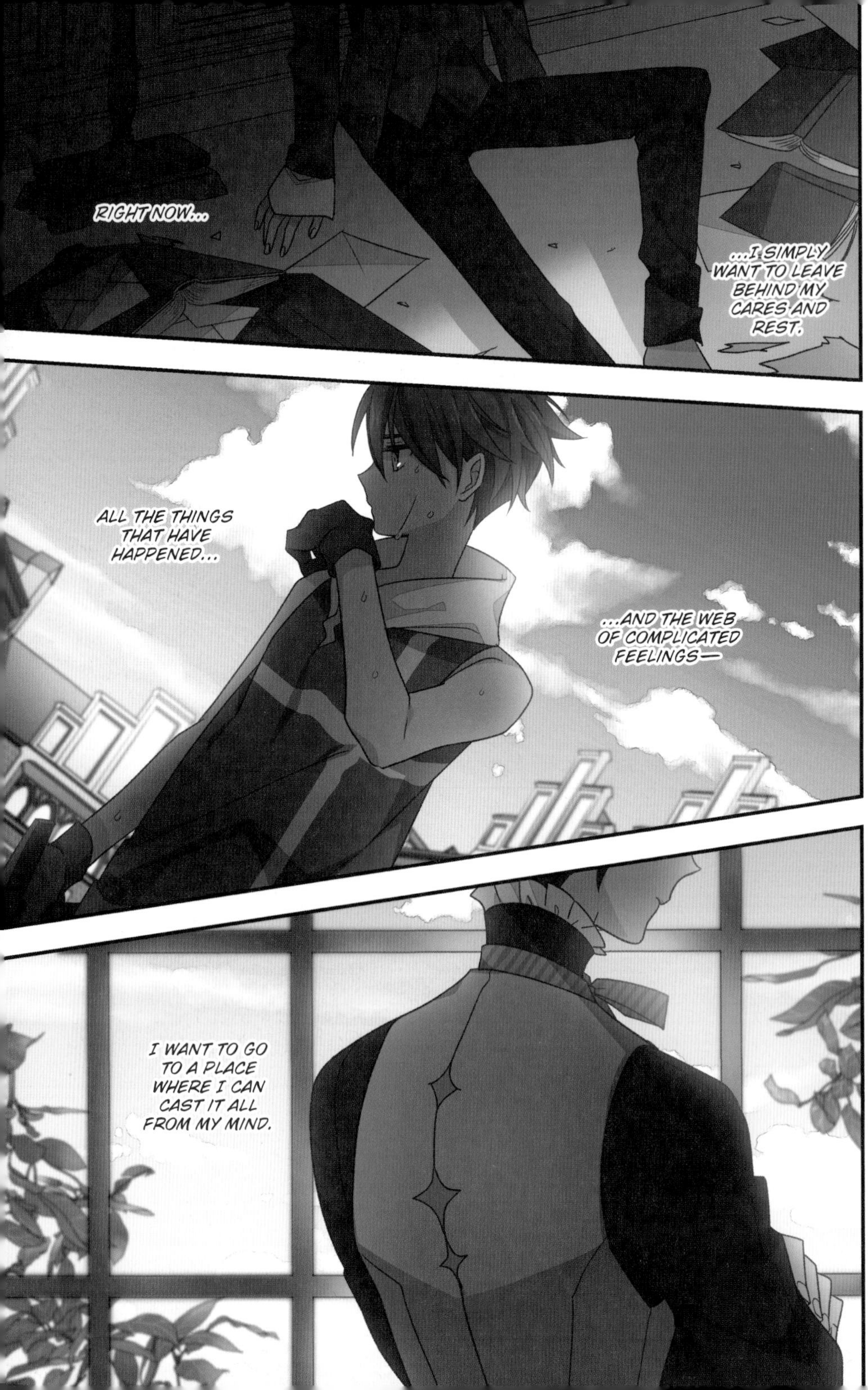
RIGHT NOW...
...I SIMPLY WANT TO LEAVE BEHIND MY CARES AND REST.
ALL THE THINGS THAT HAVE HAPPENED...
...AND THE WEB OF COMPLICATED FEELINGS—
I WANT TO GO TO A PLACE WHERE I CAN CAST IT ALL FROM MY MIND.

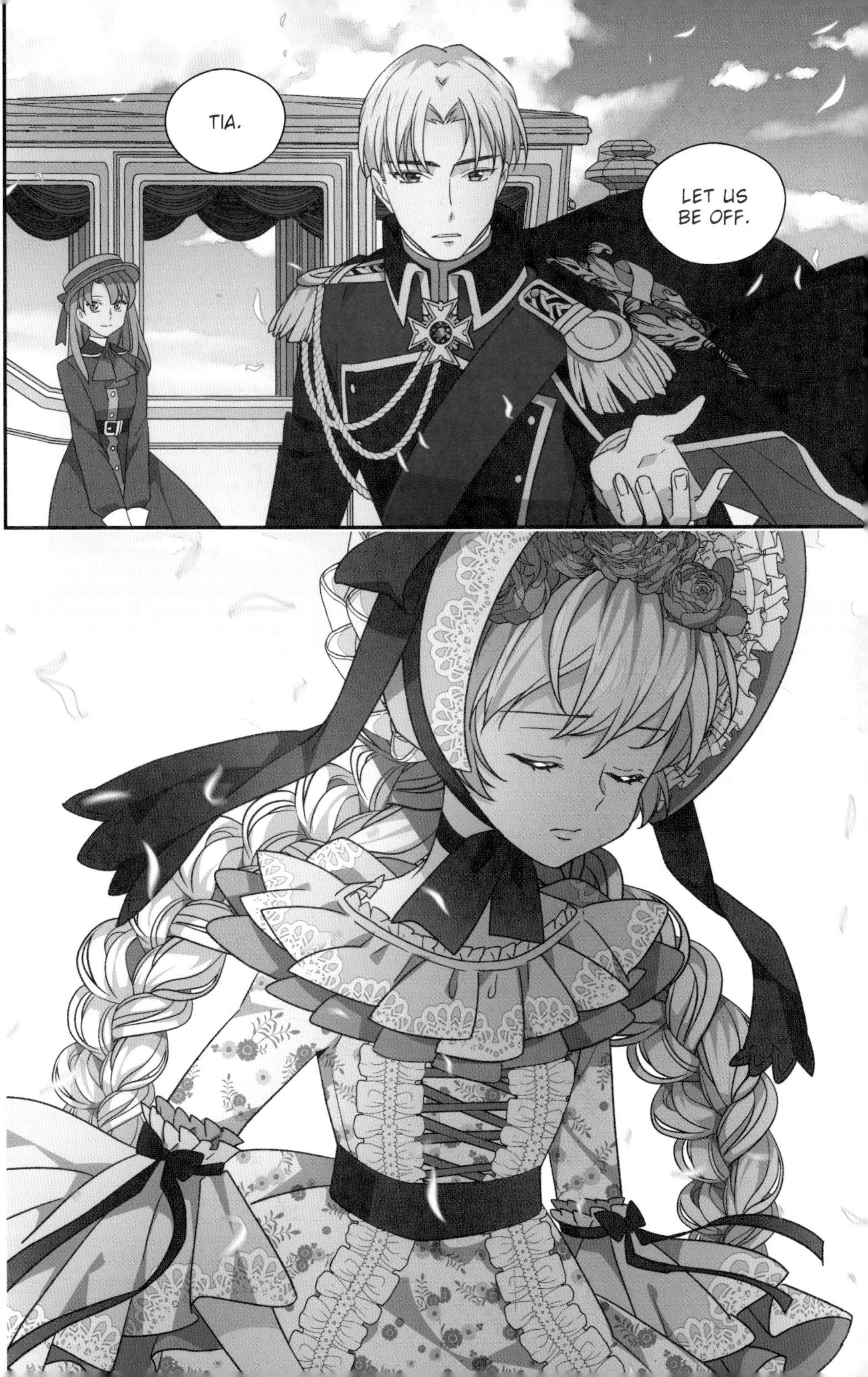
TIA.
LET US BE OFF.

TO A PLACE
FAR, FAR FROM
THE CAPITAL.

The Abandoned Empress

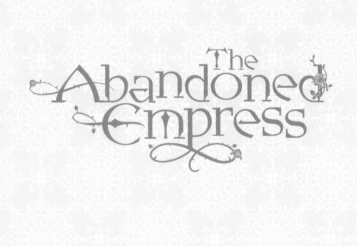

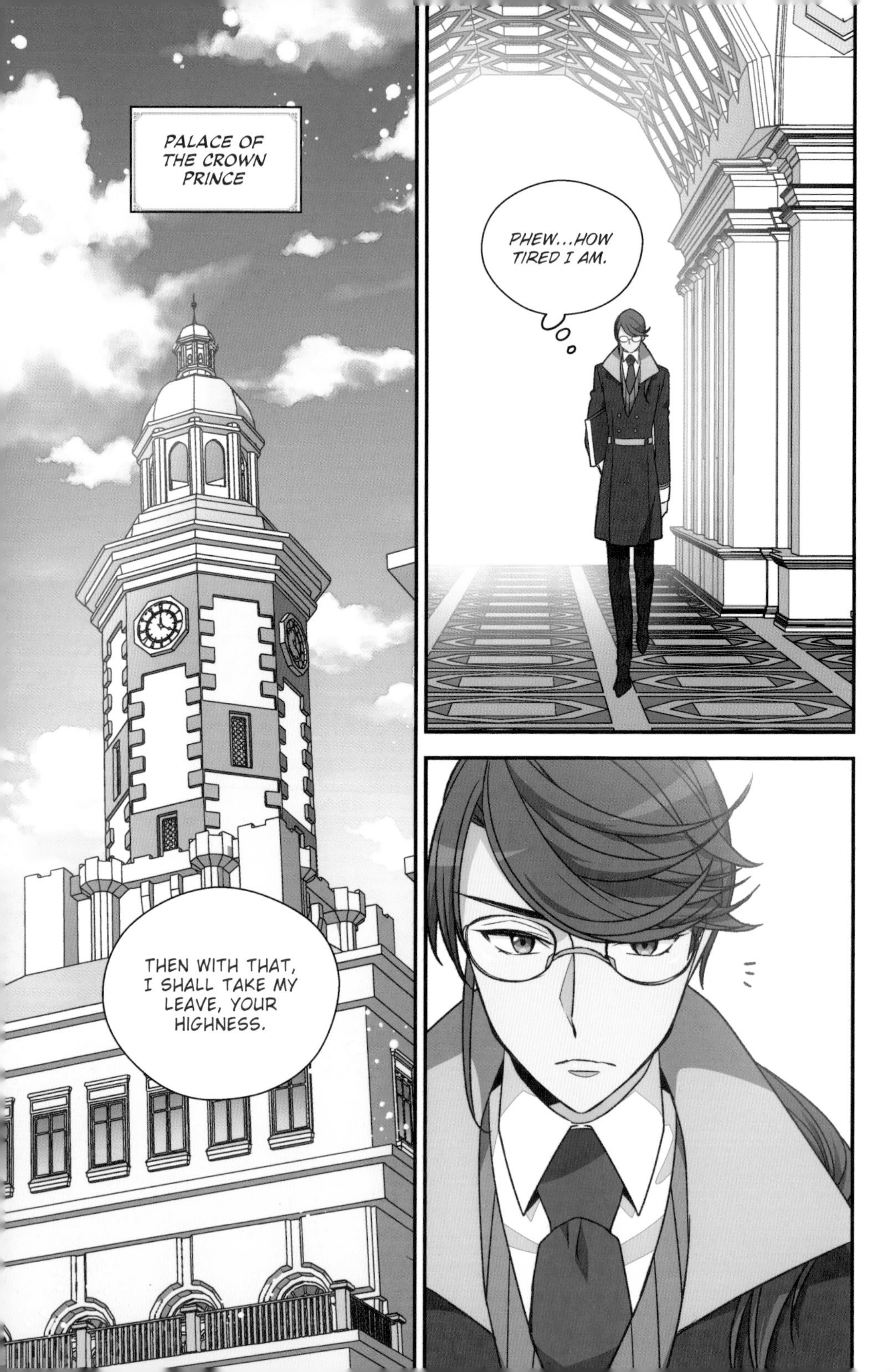
PALACE OF THE CROWN PRINCE
THEN WITH THAT, I SHALL TAKE MY LEAVE, YOUR HIGHNESS.
PHEW...HOW TIRED I AM.

ARKINT.

AH, ALL FINISHED, ARE YOU NOW?

KEIREAN'S FLITTED OFF ON VACATION, I HEAR.

INDEED. IT APPEARS THEY'RE TAKING A QUAINT FATHER-DAUGHTER TRIP TO THEIR COUNTRY ABODE.

IT'S BEEN A FEW DAYS ALREADY, SO I'D RECKON THEY'VE ARRIVED BY NOW.

AND HIS MAJESTY SANCTIONED THIS ALL WITH NO ESPECIAL OBJECTION?

HE DID! AND NOW I'M LEFT HERE HAVING TO GO TO WORK EVERY SINGLE DAY!

NOT LIKE I DON'T NEED A VACATION TOO!

※COMMANDERS OF THE TWO KNIGHTS' ORDERS NORMALLY TAKE TURNS ON PALACE DUTY.

229

...AS I THOUGHT.

THERE MUST HAVE BEEN SOME TALK BETWEEN THEM ON THE DAY OF THE COMING-OF-AGE CEREMONY ABOUT THE EVENTUALITY OF BREAKING OFF THE ENGAGEMENT.

MM-HMM. WOULD'VE TRIED ASKING THEN, BUT THERE WERE TOO MANY EYES.

SOMEONE OR OTHER MUST'VE CAUGHT WIND.

...THE NOBLIST FACTION MUST HAVE AS WELL...

AND HOW IS HIS HIGHNESS AMIDST ALL THIS?

HE IS DISCONTENT, AS YOU'D IMAGINE.

NOW THAT IT'S BEEN BROUGHT TO HIS ATTENTION...

...I WOULDN'T EXPECT HIM TO JUST SERENELY LET IT PASS HIM BY.

THINGS WILL START TO GET NOISY, I THINK.

FROM BOTH THE INSIDE AND OUT.

RATTLE

RATTLE

......TIA.

TIA.

...MMM... PAPA...?

YOU SHOULD WAKE UP. WE'RE NEARLY THERE.

HAVE A LOOK.

OHHH...!!

HELLO, BEN. IT'S BEEN TOO LONG. I HOPE LOOKING AFTER THE PLACE HASN'T TROUBLED YOU TOO MUCH.

GRANDPA BEN! HAVE YOU BEEN WELL?

WELCOME, MASTER AND THE YOUNG MISS.

NOW, WHAT TROUBLE WOULD MINDING AN EMPTY HOUSE BE TO AN OLD MAN IN HIS RETIREMENT, SIR?

MORE THAN ANYTHING, SEEING THE TWO OF YOU IN GOOD HEALTH PUTS MY MIND AT EASE.

YOU MUST BE ROAD-WEARY, THOUGH, SO LET US ATTEND TO THAT FIRST.

THIS PLACE LIES ALONG THE OUTERMOST LINE OF DEFENSE FOR THE CAPITAL.

I'D NEVER ONCE TAKEN A TRIP OR ANYTHING LIKE THIS.

WE'RE NOT THAT FAR AWAY FROM THE CAPITAL, YET IT'S SO PEACEFUL.

SUCH A DIFFERENT VISTA FROM THE CITY...

AN OLD CASTLE SWATHED IN IVY...

...AND AN EXPANSE OF TREES AND FLOWERS...

IT FEELS AS THOUGH I'M ON THE RUN.

THREE YEARS OF STRUGGLE TO WALK A PATH DIFFERENT FROM THE PAST...

...JUST TO END UP CASTING IT ALL ASIDE TO FLEE.

ESCAPING IN THIS MANNER MIGHT BE THE WRONG COURSE OF ACTION.

BUT THERE WAS NO OTHER WAY BEFORE ME.

IF PAPA HADN'T COME BACK AT THE MOMENT HE DID, I'D BE IN A MUCH BIGGER MESS.

PAPA...

SPEAKING OF, THAT EXCHANGE BETWEEN PAPA AND THE EMPEROR...

I WONDER WHAT IT ALL MEANT?

EVER SO LOVELY A VIEW, IS IT NOT?

GRANDPA BEN.

I HAD NO IDEA AT ALL THAT OUR HOUSE'S ESTATES INCLUDED SUCH A MAGNIFICENT CASTLE.

'TWAS BESTOWED BY THE IMPERIAL FAMILY SOME GENERATIONS AGO.

IT'LL SOON FIND A WELCOME PLACE IN THE YOUNG MISS'S HEART AS WELL.

IT IS UNIQUELY CALM AND QUIET HERE WHEN MEASURED AGAINST OTHER REGIONS ALONG THE BORDERS.

YES...

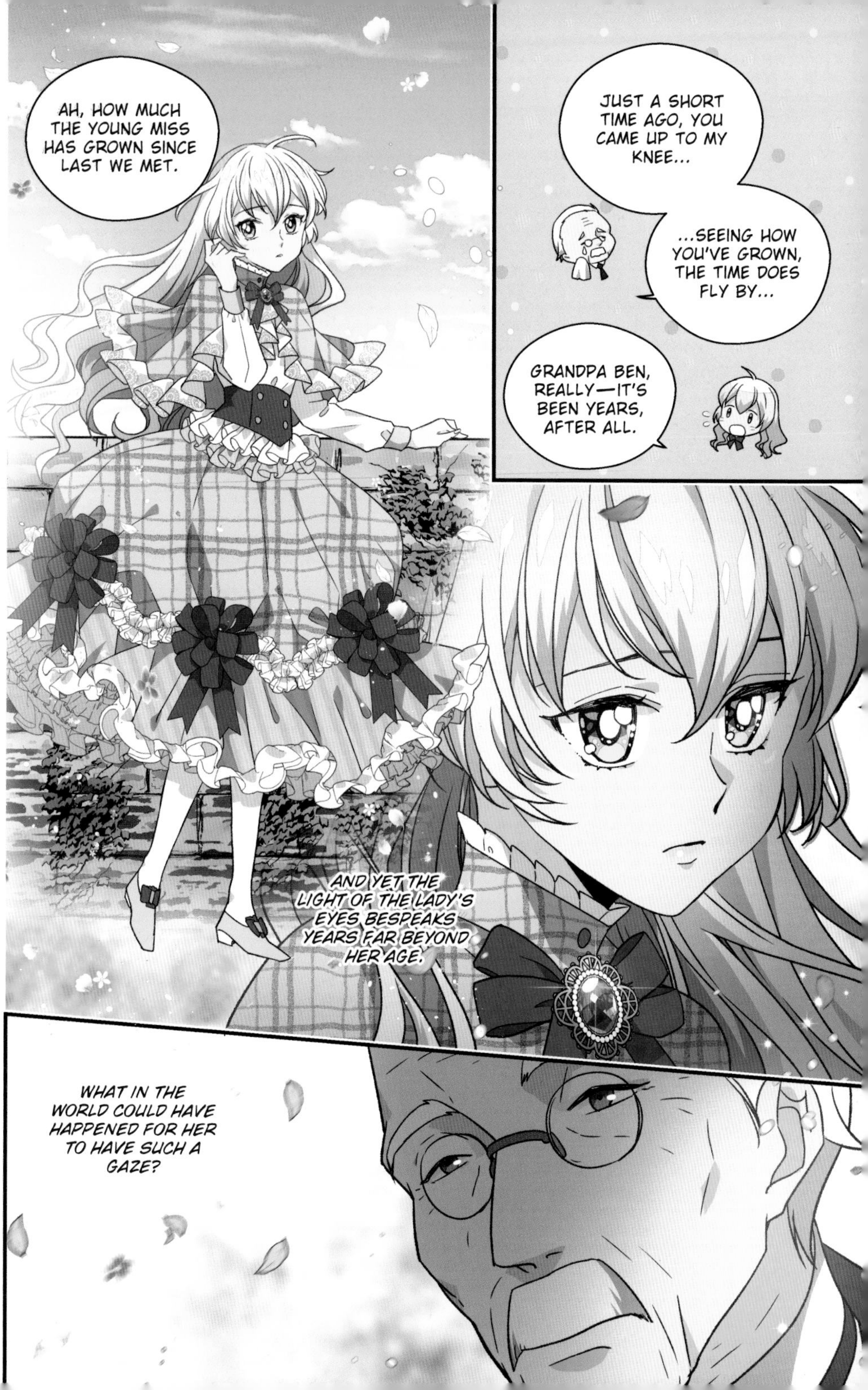
AH, HOW MUCH THE YOUNG MISS HAS GROWN SINCE LAST WE MET.
JUST A SHORT TIME AGO, YOU CAME UP TO MY KNEE...
...SEEING HOW YOU'VE GROWN, THE TIME DOES FLY BY...
GRANDPA BEN, REALLY—IT'S BEEN YEARS, AFTER ALL.
AND YET THE LIGHT OF THE LADY'S EYES BESPEAKS YEARS FAR BEYOND HER AGE.
WHAT IN THE WORLD COULD HAVE HAPPENED FOR HER TO HAVE SUCH A GAZE?

WELL, IT APPEARS AS THOUGH MY SON'S INEFFECTUALITY HAS LEFT THE YOUNG MISS WANTING FOR PROPER CARE.

ME?!

DISQUIET FILLS THE YOUNG LADY'S FACE.

I MUST ASK THE MASTER TO SEE HE'S PROPERLY CHASTISED.

OH, TH-THAT'S NOT IT! ALAN HAS BEEN PERFORMING PERFECTLY WELL!

IT'S ONLY THAT I'M TIRED FROM BEING A BIT BUSY OF LATE!

AND PAPA—

"PAPA"?

......

...FATHER NEEDS HIS REST, HAVING JUST RETURNED FROM THE CAMPAIGN.

THE MASTER AND YOUNG MISS SEEMED TO BE CLOSER THAN EVER, SO THERE'S NAUGHT ELSE TO BE DESIRED.

I'LL GO AND TELL THE OTHERS TO READY YOUR EVENING MEAL. PLEASE MAKE YOUR WAY DOWN AT YOUR LEISURE.

ALL RIGHT...

...HE SAID THAT I'VE...

...GROWN...

IT'S STILL QUITE A WAYS OFF.

I WISH WE COULD GROW UP QUICKLY, MY LADY.

WOULD YOU KNOW HOW PAINSTAKINGLY I WEIGHED YOUR ASKING ME TO TRUST YOU...

...AND HOW MY HEART COLLAPSED ON SEEING THE CYNICISM IN YOUR FACE?

WOULD YOU UNDERSTAND, ALLENDIS?

HOW MUCH THE REALITY THAT I'D BEEN CAST ASIDE ONCE AGAIN BY ONE I HAD TREASURED SO...

...HOW MUCH IT...

YOUNG MISS!!

COME DOWN AND TAKE A LOOK!!

IT'S A WHOLE BED OF BLOOMING FLOWERS ON WHEELS!

...I'M ON MY WAY.

I DON'T WANT TO THINK OF ANY OF IT RIGHT NOW.

241

I'LL TURN MY EYES TOWARD WHAT BRINGS MY HEART HAPPINESS...

...AND REST TO MY HEART'S CONTENT.

AFTER ALL, THAT'S WHY I'M HERE...

REGARDLESS
OF THE FACT
THAT OTHERS
MIGHT POINT
THEIR FINGERS
AND ACCUSE ME
OF FLEEING.

...TIA.

The Abandoned Empress

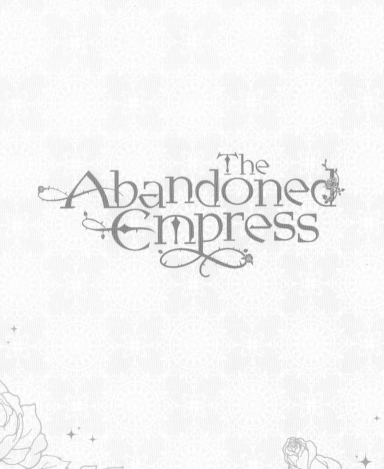

◆ VOLUME 4 PREVIEW ◆

YOU SAW THEM THAT DAY TOO.

THE TWO OF THEM, THE NIGHT OF HIS COMING OF AGE?

Allendis seeks to keep Ruve in check.

Carsein's feelings start to get complicated.

...BECAUSE OF THE TERROR SHE FEELS OF ME?

Ruve grows frustrated, unable to understand Tia's choice.

In the end, the crown prince
decides to pay Tia a visit...

And Tia discovers a new
opportunity!

Volume 4 Out 2022!

The Abandoned Empress

INA
Original Story by Yuna

Translation: DAVID ODELL   Lettering: LYS BLAKESLEE

THE ABANDONED EMPRESS Volume 3
© INA, Yuna 2017 / D&C WEBTOON Biz
All rights reserved.
First published in Korea in 2017 by D&C WEBTOON Biz Co., Ltd.

English translation © 2022 by Yen Press, LLC

Yen Press
150 West 30th Street, 19th Floor
New York, NY 10001

Visit us at yenpress.com
facebook.com/yenpress
twitter.com/yenpress
yenpress.tumblr.com
instagram.com/yenpress

First Yen Press Edition: September 2022
Edited by Yen Press Editorial: Won Young Seo, JuYoun Lee
Designed by Yen Press Design: Wendy Chan

Yen Press is an imprint of Yen Press, LLC.
The Yen Press name and logo are trademarks of Yen Press, LLC.

Library of Congress Control Number: 2021943164

ISBNs: 978-1-9753-3730-8 (paperback)
978-1-9753-3731-5 (ebook)

1 3 5 7 9 10 8 6 4 2

TPA

Printed in South Korea